CAMP FOLLOWER

ONE ARMY BRAT'S STORY

Michele Sabad

HTTPS://STEVIESZABAD.COM/

Cover art, design, and interior sketches by Caro Fréchette.
Typesetting and interior design by Éric Desmarais.
Edited by Cait Gordon.
Author photo by Ryan Sabad

Legal deposit, Library and Archives Canada, October 2017.

Paperback ISBN: 978-1-7751423-0-0
Ebook ISBN: 978-1-7751423-1-7

MESabad
https://stevieszabad.com/

Dedicated to the memory of my mother,
Myrtle Sabad.

CONTENTS

PREFACE

Spring 1999: Aylmer, Québec

"Okay, boys, we're going to Germany for holidays this year! Right after school lets out in June," my husband Don announces.

"Huh?" says D'Arcy, my soon-to-turn thirteen-year-old son.

"What? Why Germany?" asks his nine-year-old brother, Sasha.

"Yeah, why not Disneyworld or something? And aren't we going to Manitoba in August? Where did you come up with Germany?"

Why Germany indeed? My husband Don and I, both army brats who had lived in Germany as kids, had recently realized that our own rapidly-growing children had not really lived or been anywhere other than their own province of Québec. Sure, they'd been born in Winnipeg and visited Manitoba to see grandparents every summer, but gosh, by the time I was nine I'd lived in two different countries, and by thirteen I could add a couple more different provinces as having been my home. Same for my husband. Despite Don's being an Air Force officer himself, our kids were not really military brats—not like we had been. When had the world changed? Why had I not noticed?

Well, it's a long story. My story.

INTRODUCTION

If you grew up in the 1960s or 1970s on Canadian military bases, then maybe joined up yourself or became a military spouse, I know a few things about you. First, you don't have a hometown. Sorry, it doesn't matter where you were born; it's not a hometown if you don't remember it or have no family in it. I know you would have explained this countless times to people over the years in response to the innocently asked, "Where are you from?" and, "Oh, you moved around with the military? But where were you born?"

Take a deep breath; explain it again.

Another thing I know is that you're very patriotic. You cry at the national anthem anytime, anywhere: community events, hockey or ball games (even those on TV), not to mention at Canada or Remembrance Day or any kind of ceremony—especially if there are bagpipes! You are attuned to anything military, like news headlines or TV shows. You stop and look up wistfully at the droning Hercules flying overhead, or better yet, thrill to the random F-18 jet flyby. You probably touch, even fondle the tank now sitting as a monument in your town's armoury square.

You might get itchy to move every couple of years, or, conversely, never want to move ever again. I do know you feel connected as a community to others who shared your upbringing. You make new acquaintances, to find out they grew up military and the immediate rapport is: "Where were you posted? Me too! When did you live there? Did you know so-and-so?"

You know the drill. Pun intended.

Of course, these things I know, too; it's also my story.

I didn't have a hometown, but I do have half or maybe three-quarters of a lifetime of stories about the sub-culture of people attached to the Canadian Armed Forces. I lived the life of a base brat—also known as a military brat; PMQ brat; Army, Navy, or Air Force brat (all terms to describe us)—and our unique lifestyle, which was the lifestyle of the Camp Follower.

There have been camp followers ever since humanity has sent people—historically men—off to fight wars on behalf of the societies, cultures, or countries they represent. The camp followers provided services to the fighting men: food, supplies, tailoring, housekeeping, entertainment, even the "comfort" that women have always found men willing to pay for. A whole camp-follower community would pop up outside the fenced, permanent military camp or base, which existed as its own small town. In Canada today, the camp-follower lifestyle is much more integrated into the civilian world, but you can find such towns still economically dependent on the military base they once grew around, such as Courtenay, British Columbia; Oromocto, New Brunswick; and Petawawa, Ontario.

Camp followers have also always included immediate families of the warrior member. Soldiers, sailors, and airmen are people, and these people love, marry, and procreate. The modern military, as in after World War II, formally institutionalized this reality with Personal Married Quarters (PMQ) for the married member. We called our homes PMQs more often than "houses."

As the old Canadian Armed Forces recruitment slogan said: *There's no life like it*—even for the camp follower. Well, there had been no life like it, but that lifestyle has mostly melted away today. Historically speaking, we live in peaceful times, where our military members are highly educated and well-paid. They are more likely to buy a house in the civilian community than to put their family in a rented PMQ. The Department of National Defence (DND) school system is dismantled and military kids go to civilian schools. Postings are for longer periods today, and family considerations are respected. The old base-brat experience that I knew has pretty much expired.

I grew up in different times for our country and its armed forces: post-WWII and Allied bases in Europe, the Cold War, peacekeeping missions in Cyprus and the Middle East. My father joined the army to escape poverty, not as a career choice to get a trained skill that he could use in civilian life later. It was a unique time in history, with unique experiences for those who lived it. And it was brief, only lasting really a generation, more or less. It was also the generation of the Baby Boomers, which had its own uniqueness in Western society. Coupled with a military upbringing, this base-brat experience was doubly unique for people like me.

We lived on military bases in PMQs that were assigned and not chosen, based on family size and member's rank. We went to DND schools. As dependent spouses and children, we were issued our own ID cards for access to our gated and fenced (barb-wired) communities. We learned to read "Defense de Passer" on the signs of our delineated borders. No matter where we were, the base was always bilingual as far as I remember. We were subject to search and seizure at any time, for any reason, by the military police. We had curfews. Our school buses were army green and driven by uniformed privates or corporals. And the interesting part? We didn't think anything about this life was out of the ordinary. It was ordinary to us—we were born into it, not recruited or chosen. Yet ordinary it was not. It is not ordinary to grow up never living among elderly people, or people with special needs. It is not ordinary to hand over ID on command as a teenager to military police "just because." It is not ordinary to move multiple times in the same school year, or live out of a motel while your furniture catches up. Or never live in the same town as your relatives, to never meet some grandparents. Not to say that these things never happened in civilian life—of course they did. I'm just saying that *all* of these kinds of things and more happened to *most* base brats of my time.

We all usually caught up with the reality of the rest of the world at some point, and most of us eventually integrated well with that world. But as all children do, the adults we became carried this base-brat upbringing with us, sometimes for good, sometimes not.

All of this to say that we camp followers may not have been members in the military, but we sure as hell lived our own version of a military life.

Which is the story of my own life, and I'm not alone. I've seen statistics (in Wikipedia) from the US that put the number of adults living today who grew up as base brats at over 10 million. In Canada, this number is smaller of course, but to me it always meant that although we weren't from anywhere in particular, we were all from the same community; it just happened to be spread across the country, and over other countries, too, like the United States, Germany, or France.

Your base-brat experiences are likely similar to my own. We might never have had a hometown, but we had a home culture.

And if you weren't a base brat, welcome to our world! Believe me, your stories of life in one place, while normal for you, never fail to impress me. As I've settled and retired to the real civilian world, I experience shock if I see a store close that I remember opening, or see a young man all grown up that I knew as a childhood friend of my son. I never experienced the march of change in place until now, decades into life in my adopted hometown of Aylmer, Québec. Life happens everywhere. We all get there in the end. It's the stories that we live and share along the way that make things interesting.

These stories of transplantation and the military are mine; they describe as faithfully as memory allows. They are meant to be entertaining and enlightening about a kind of lifestyle that existed briefly in our Canadian history, by one who experienced it firsthand. They are not meant to be fact-checked for exact dates, locations, or names. This is not a history reference book. I have kept to the truth as much as possible, and where not, I take care to clarify where and why not. I hope the stories portrayed are not seen as just my stories, but stories of a type of base-brat life. An ordinary life, but one where the lessons we all collect were, in my case, coloured and influenced by being a Canadian camp follower.

PART ONE. AN ARMY CHILDHOOD.

FAMILY AND COUNTRY

My younger son Sasha, while still a teenager, once mentioned in a moment of maturity that he considered himself one of the most fortunate people in the world because he'd been born in Canada. It shocked me, such an observation. His reflection crystalized an obvious fact of my own life. I'd also been born in Canada, and even luckier, I'd been born into a military family.

We all come from somewhere. I was only an army brat because my father joined the Army. My father enlisted because his family were prairie farmers and he didn't want to farm. This little vignette, although fanciful in the author's depiction, recounts true facts about my grandmother and her first husband. Her story reminds me of how lucky I really am that my father didn't stay on the farm!

Peter felt the first pain, a twinge in his side, while tossing feed. The barn was small—just the two milk cows, the old sow, the chickens—but cozy, an oasis of life. Outside, the wicked white prairie winter blanketed the rich sleeping earth—farmland that he, Peter, and other homesteaders wrestled into expansion year by year.

He walked across the yard, sloshing steaming milk that froze into pellets as it spilled, eager for the hearty breakfast Mabel was making for him and the hired man coming from his father's today. They would finish clearing for the laneway while the land was still hard, and before the threatening snowstorm hit. Peter wanted that Model T this year, first one in the district. Mabel was well and pregnant with their third child, and their oldest son David was already helpful with chores. But now the pain stabbed again; Peter gasped and struggled to the house.

Later, blizzard raging, Peter lay in bed, sweating in and out of consciousness. More angry than afraid, both he and Mabel knew his appendix must have burst. The laneway was still impassable.

Holding his wife's hand, slipping away to relief, he said, "Mabel, I don't know how you're going to make it."

But my grandmother did make it. She would go on to run the farm outside of Killarney, Manitoba for a couple of years herself, with help from her husband's family. And then she would marry again to a Hungarian immigrant six years her junior and have three more children: their eldest son Kenneth being one of them—Ken, my father. My father who joined the Army.

1962: KINGSTON, ONTARIO. AN EARLY LESSON.

A lthough one brother and I were born in Calgary, Alberta, my first memories are of Kingston, Ontario, where we lived between two postings to Calgary, my parents adding another brother upon each move. What follows is a little memory of that time. Although my mother taught me that "People are all different but everyone is equal and should be treated equally", even she could be kind to a fault!

"Now Mickey honey, you have to give the paintbrush to Emily . . . she's deaf!" This last part whispered by her mother.

But four-year old Michele, who insisted her name was really Mickey—she could even spell it from the TV show: "M-I-C-K-E-Y M-O-U-S-E, MICKEY MOUSE!"— was having none of it. What did being deaf have to do with anything, anyway? She'd found the paintbrush, bristles lush and black and shiny, in perfect condition on the vacant lot around the corner from the big Victorian house where her family lived in the converted upstairs apartment. Why her dad hadn't got them into PMQs in Kingston, she didn't know, but it was probably because he didn't have enough points yet. The Army would allocate housing based on how long the soldier had been married and how many children he had, so this creaky apartment was a cheap alternative while her parents racked up the marriage years and added more family brothers. Mickey didn't mind. The neighbourhood was near a giant park, where her father would take her and her year-younger brother Mark after work to chase and retrieve his golf balls. Dad was teaching himself how to golf from the right side instead of his natural left, "Because courses are built for righties," he used to say.

There were also numerous empty garbage-filled lots where old houses were coming down, just begging to be explored and plundered. They were stinky and unattended with no new construction going on that Mickey ever remembered seeing. Her mother called the neighbourhood "Down and Going," whatever that meant.

In the meantime, after lunch when Mom was usually napping with Mark and the new baby, Mickey occupied herself until Dad came home with outside adventures, such as treasure-hunting in the scrubby-empty-lot land. Often she would call on the girl from across the street, Emily, to join her. That Emily couldn't talk very clearly, and needed to be shown things rather than told, didn't hinder their expeditions. They had strict rules forbidding them from playing in the lots, though. Mickey painfully remembered stepping on a nail there once, to come home limping and bleeding. Summers were spent barefoot. She thought the even more painful immersion into the pot of boiled, salty water to clean it had been more punishment than the bloody foot itself.

But today, rules forgotten as they will be to a four-year old's reasoning, the girls hadn't been able to resist the new hill of plowed stuff they'd seen, and set to it immediately. They weren't disappointed. This hill was loaded and strewn with riches: paper sacks folded and not even soiled, a remarkable long yellow pencil with the lead still sharp, a pair (*a pair!*) of men's socks, and finally, a polished wooden-handled paintbrush, not the kiddie kind for crafts, but big and real for painting walls. The silky thick bristles were spotless and soft on Mickey's cheek; the tool looked like it could still be hanging in the hardware store. Mickey held it up for Emily to admire.

"MAY!" Emily shouted. Mickey stood up from her crouch.

"No, I found it. It's mine!" But Emily was reaching for it and repeated, "May! May! *Maaay!*"

This wasn't going well. Mickey jumped up, leaving the pencil and paper bags where they were. Clutching the thick handle of the paintbrush, she ran as fast as her bare little feet would go—careless of watching her step—out of the lot, down the cracked sidewalk all the way up her porch steps, and through the wooden screen door on the landing, where she paused just long enough to latch the little metal hook on the inside so Emily couldn't follow her in. Because Emily *had* followed, and Mickey had made it inside just in time.

Emily banged on the door and howled, "May! MAY!"

Obviously the yelling and banging and thumping up the stairs to the upstairs landing brought Mickey's mother out.

"*Michele*, take that mangy paintbrush back downstairs and give it to Emily, the poor thing! Right now!"

Poor thing? Deaf? Mickey did not understand. But as her

mother stood one hand on hip pointing sternly down the stairs, Mickey noticed Emily had quieted down and was standing back, hands neatly folded in front of her grubby play dress, waiting like an angel for Mickey the devil-child to hand over the goods.

Mickey complied with a sulk, stomping back down the stairs and unlatching the door. Emily grinned. And as Mickey's mother turned to leave the landing upstairs, her parental duty accomplished, Emily hugged the paintbrush close and stuck out her tongue. A gesture which Mickey returned in kind.

Turns out years later I searched for that old Victorian house in Kingston on Division Street, but over time it and all the vacant lots had melded into the ever-expanding campus buildings of Queen's University. I wonder where Emily ended up? I bet she did okay. Little did I know it then, but she would be the only person with special needs that I would ever meet in childhood, since after this time in Kingston, I'd live on military bases until I left home. Emily taught me that everybody should be treated the same, regardless of differences. A good first lesson. In years to come, I would encounter many different people in many different places, and tried to remember. Mostly I did.

Nov 22, 1963: CFB Calgary

Military families learn early that world events have direct consequences on their personal lives. This memory of an influential historic event is as true as I and my father can recall.

Mickey's story

I'm five years old, living in our PMQ row-house in Calgary. Usually my army Dad was at work on base. He was a Physical Training Instructor, so he worked at the gym when he wasn't out running the troops. At this time he was on course in Borden, Ontario, and had been gone since September, just a month or so after we had moved to Calgary from Kingston. I was supposed to have started school that fall, but by moving we had missed registration and kindergarten was full. This was a great annoyance to me, since I had been eagerly anticipating school. Instead I hung out with my four-year-old brother, Mark, drawing or watching TV in the quiet morning hours after chores, and before lunch. My mother was quite young then, not yet 25, and had dark hair and eyes with white creamy skin that would burn in the shade. She would be busy with my baby brother and preparing for afternoon errands, like walking for groceries, or to the bank, or post office. We didn't own a car.

Most details about that day in Calgary—what we had for breakfast, what we had planned for the day's outing, or even the weather—I cannot recall. We were a typical military family, young and busy, even somewhat poor, although that was never an issue on bases where we all shared that lifestyle. Even my often-absent father was just the norm for me and my friends.

No, what I remember that one November day is being in the kitchen, colouring at the chrome dinette, and then suddenly hearing my mother cry out from the living room. I paused, startled and concerned. What dreadful interruption on the TV had made her jump up from her morning cigarette? (I hated washing ashtrays.) My mother had jumped up from the tatty sofa and stumbled back to the hallway towards the kitchen, still staring at the black and white screen, where she reached for the beige rotary wall phone. Ignoring me, her pretty face wrinkled and scrunched up as I rarely saw, I guessed she must have tried calling my father. But no, he was away, and not available except by letters. In those days even an emergency phone call would have had to go through the base chaplain. It was 1963.

*W*hat my father remembered of that moment was this, and I will let him speak in his own words.

KEN'S STORY

I was finishing my twelve-week Senior Leaders course in Borden, and we were on parade. It was a Friday after lunch, and we awaited final inspection and presentation of our graduation certificates. With this qualification I would now be eligible for promotion to Sergeant. The course had been brutally physical and tough; most of us were looking forward to a party night to say so long to our buddies before we got on trains to nurse inevitable hangovers on long rides back to our various military bases—Calgary for me. But as we stood at attention, the lieutenant from Headquarters, without any of the usual decorum, ran over the parade square directly to the colonel in front of our platoon.

After a frozen moment, we heard the CO exclaim, "You're shitting me!"

I cannot ever recall hearing the old man, as we called him, swear. I felt a sweaty chill in the cold November air. The officers talked some more, then the CO turned to us, still formed up, and spoke. To this very day, I remember exactly what he said.

"President Kennedy has just been assassinated. You are to return to barracks and pack up. You will be bused to trains immediately and returned to home units, where you will await further orders. Dismissed!"

Then he turned and hurried away with the lieutenant.

We stood stunned, before running back to barracks, our minds numb. We were in the middle of a Cold War with the Russians; I thought this was the start of WWIII. What else could I think—I was in the Army! Climbing aboard the train later that afternoon, though, I wistfully thought of the missed after-course blowout party. Certificates were sent on later. I don't remember how or when I got mine, but I do recall that I was presented with my sergeant's hooks before that very Christmas.

I never did find out who my mother phoned to share the shock of that day. My aunt says my mother didn't phone home to Manitoba. Probably it was another young wife in our PMQ block that she had befriended. It was a heart-breaking week; I remember watching the nonstop televised coverage for quite a few days, weeping with my mother, holding my brother's hand, despite not fully understanding then what the beloved American president had meant to the whole world in that time of history. I can only guess now what terrifying thoughts his death then must have conjured for an army wife—thoughts of her husband going to war?

My beautiful mother died of lung cancer in 1999, the same week that Jack Jr. was killed in a plane crash. I still feel somehow comforted that the Kennedy family and my own, at the same time, shared such grief. Again.

Riches and fame don't shield anyone from the ordinary consequences of life. Lessons being learned, my childhood was starting to feel military, whatever that meant to a little girl.

1965: Santa is Real

When my father was posted to Germany in 1965, we were supposed to move in the summer with the rest of his Battalion. But the latest baby brother had severe eczema and couldn't get his vaccination shots until he was cleared. So, we moved at Christmas instead. Lesson on this one: It's only with the passing of years that we can fully appreciate how much our parents did for us kids. What an example this memory is.

Mom says not to worry; Santa knows where we are all the time. No matter that we're moving to Germany three days before Christmas. He'll find us, she promises. I'm not convinced. She already gave away our dog Max. She says he can't fly on a plane and that he'll love his new life on the farm.

I don't like my Grade 2 teacher here at Sarcee Elementary, anyway. She won't let me read the books on the shelf at the back of the room when I've already finished the baby ones she gave us, so I don't care that we're moving. I just mind that we couldn't put a tree up for Christmas. And that my Malibu Barbie with bendable legs is in the Eaton's store here, in Calgary. How do I know if Santa can find the exact same one in Unna, Germany?

"Goodbye Canada," I say from the airplane. It's so blue

in the sky and so white down on the ground as we take off. I hope Mom packed my ice skates. It was just getting cold enough to use them in the townhouse courtyard back home. Well, back at the old Calgary home.

Not that long later, Dad is calling, "Look out the window, kids, there's Germany. We're landing!"

But it's not white here. It's dark green on the ground and grey in the sky. Cold, but in that chilly way that shivers through your sweater, not the kind of crispy blue cold that I like, the kind where you can go skating in the front courtyard. The pouring rain heavily drums me to sleep on the bus ride to our new town, on winding shiny black roads that are crowded on the sides with strangely tall trees. It doesn't feel like Christmas at all—maybe it's not Christmas in Germany? Mom still says not to worry, but I'm suspicious. She's busy hauling her heavy suitcase and my baby brother. She tells me to make sure my other brothers Mark and John aren't fighting. Where is the snow? I don't see any Christmas lights in the dark when we show up at our new home. It's just a tall, ugly square building and I don't see any courtyard. My brothers are pinching each other, but Dad pulls them apart. They race inside leaving Dad to bellow after them to come back for their bags.

As big sister and only girl, I get my own room in our new German apartment. There's a bed and desk already there, even blankets and pillows. I unpack my suitcase and sit on the bed. There. All moved in.

Mom is digging through boxes in the living room. I don't know what she brought—what else do we need? The apartment has a couch and chairs and dishes and everything. No TV, I notice. I sit and read comic books with my brothers. Mom unwraps the family platter that the Christmas, Easter, and Thanksgiving turkeys sit on. Is it Christmas tomorrow? I don't have high hopes. We still don't have a tree. My brothers fight over the comic books, oblivious. Am I the only one who remembers the date? It's supposed to be Christmas!

We do wake up early the next morning and there is a little bush of a tree set up and I do recognize the old glass bulb ornaments and tinsel. Where did they come from? Dad's army socks are plump full on the unfamiliar couch, and tearing into them my brothers and I each find an orange and candy, which we're allowed to eat before breakfast. Then I look; there are things under the tree. Not wrapped but . . . I see bright plastic toy cars, a hockey stick, a wagon, and then there it is—the big square box with the plastic window front. It's my Malibu Barbie, all tanned and bendable and just exactly the right one! Mom was right; Santa did find us!

My mother Myrtle carried the heirloom serving platter that she inherited from her own grandmother, who was from a Scottish-heritage homesteading family, in her suitcase on every move. She never trusted the movers and she was right not to. The storage company in Calgary, where our furniture and possessions had been kept while we were in Germany and then Goose Bay, had gone bankrupt by the time we would get them. More than half of our family's possessions were never retrieved. I remember I did get back some dolls and other babyish items left in storage by seven-year-old me, which the by-then twelve-year-old Michele didn't want or need any more.

1965-1968: Foreign Life

*C*hildhood in Germany. Where to begin? My army father posted to Iserlohn at Christmas from Calgary, Alberta. We lived in fully-furnished military housing in the nearby town of Unna, which today is part of Dortmund in the Ruhr Valley. My brother Mark and I went to the same school in another nearby town of Werl, I starting there in the middle of grade two and he in grade one. It was another first day of school, and over the span of our lives as Canadian military base brats, it wouldn't be the last. The previous "first day" had been in Calgary, when I started in grade one while he got to start in kindergarten. But here's the story of my and Mark's preparation for this first day at the DND School of Werl, Germany. I was just beginning my life as caretaker to my brothers, so I can be forgiven the slight SNAFU (Situation Normal All F—ed Up) from time to time. Like this one.

"Mark, get up! It's time to go to school," I tried to whisper as I shook him. It was still night-dark and I didn't want to wake the two other brothers sharing the room. Mark got up and I showed him the pile of new school clothes to put on. It was to be our first day going to Werl DND, and we had to catch a bus. Christmas vacation over, we'd moved to Germany about a week ago. Or so I thought; it was hard to keep track of the days. They'd been dark, and busy, and timeless since arriving, what with Christmas and meeting other kids in the building and exploring the new neighbourhood and all. Nonstop rain the whole time. So different from the clear blue white-winter cold we'd left in Calgary.

While Mark joined me, patiently waiting, I looked around the new kitchen and tried to find bowls for cereal. The kitchen was huge and full of cupboards loaded with dishes and unfamiliar apparatuses, like meat grinders, mysterious utensils, and all sorts of pots and pans. But for all the searching and moving chairs to stand on, we couldn't find the cereal bowls. So, I padded out in stocking feet down the linoleum hall to my parents' room and tiptoed in to ask Mom where they were.

"What in God's name are you doing up?" Dad rolled over to roar. "It's three a.m., for Chrissake."

Mom woke and chortled a little, then went back to sleep. Dad however, continued, "And Mark's up too? For God's sake! Get back to bed. Now. Don't make me get up!"

"Okay, okay, sheesh," I said, insulted. Eager to go to school, I didn't trust my parents to wake me on time. Heck, I was often tasked with waking *them* up, especially if Dad had a golf game or something on a Saturday that he didn't want to miss by sleeping his late Friday night off. I sure didn't want to miss the bus today, so I crept back out and Mark and I just made toast and went to the living room to eat and read comic books. On the nice comfy couch. Where we both fell asleep. To be woken by our grinning mother hours later, to get up and get ready for school.

First day in a new school, kids! You don't want to miss it!

*A*nd that's how I remember starting my first day of school in Germany. Mark and I would walk down the street to the corner where we'd hang out with the cluster of other little kids and wait for the green army bus to come. It was scary fun in the fog of early-morning winter Germany. We'd run down the middle of the road for the thrill of disappearing into the ever-present chilly mist.

Mark and I started schools together all the time on our moves, and we graduated high school together later, too, because we finished in Ontario—he from Grade 12 and I from Grade 13. Our grandmother came to Ontario from Manitoba for the ceremony, and only brought a present for me because she didn't understand that Mark was graduating, too. He didn't go on to Grade 13, although he did spend another year retaking some Grade 12 classes to improve his marks, and to wait for his age to catch up, as he was still only 16 at his high school graduation. He joined the military himself a month before he turned 18. It was, and still is, true that many base kids eventually join the military themselves. Why not? It's already a familiar lifestyle.

But back to Germany.

Meanwhile, school in Germany was great, and my initial suspicions about the new world here were dissipating. As children, we do adapt to wherever we're tossed around, and I was learning to enjoy the tossing. Werl DND. It was a large school with endless wings and corridors. There were countless activities and events, like theatre plays, track and field meets, and auditorium presentations for all kinds of things. Plus, the school was mixed with both English and French classes to serve all the Canadians over there; our neighbours in Unna were French Canadian. Because I soon showed myself a talented and eager student, I was put into the bilingual stream. There was no such thing as French immersion in those days—bilingual stream simply meant that you did half your day in English and half in French. We had German classes, too. Our brownie pack was called the *Fourth Kanadisher*. I was old enough to be annoyed that the Germans spelled Canada with a K.

Summers were filled with day-camp adventures: swimming, crafts, sports, and weekly bus trips to visit tourist spots, like Hermann the German, or Altena Castle, which was nearby. A big trip would be to Cologne Cathedral, or a children's opera show in Dortmund. Some of the best times on those trips were the bus rides. Kids would be picked up from the various German towns where the Canadians had housing, places like Unna where I lived, and then Hemer, Werl, Soest, and Iserlohn. I can recite perfectly the songs we'd sing:

"We are the UNNA* girls, (* substitute HEMER or whoever screamed the loudest)
We wear our hair in curls,
We wear our dungarees way up above our knees.
We wear our father's shirts,
Instead of wearing skirts,
And when it comes to boys,
We treat them just like toys!"

Wow, talk about girl power. This was 1967. There were many other songs, most quite vulgar that we little kids weren't allowed to sing out loud, but we listened hard and learned. I guess most of these songs were old World War II ditties that the older kids picked up and modified for our times and circumstances.

My father, being the recreation director for the base kids, in addition to his day job as a military physical fitness trainer, would hire and pay the teenagers who were the counselors. They'd come to the house on paydays where my dad would dish out the marks and pfennigs. I wonder if the instructors gave my brother and I any special treatment? I don't think so, but I can't remember any bad days at summer camp, or, as we knew it, the Summer Recreation Program.

What a privileged childhood it had been for Canadian base kids to experience Europe so intimately. Most of us travelled at least a little. We went to Holland to see Madurodam, a fascinating miniature city, and stepped in the North Sea, which was too cold even for Canadians to swim in. We went to many, many castles. We shopped for bread and *brochens* (buns) in cobblestoned downtowns with huge cathedrals in central squares, and swam in expansive city pools called spas where there were mixed men and women's change rooms. But mostly we just lived our normal kid lives. We didn't think it was an extraordinary life. It was just life.

But the reality of that time was this: it was still post-World War II Germany, and only by revisiting Unna in 1999 did I fully understand how bleak and devastated Germany still was back then, just twenty years after the war. I remember as a kid riding my bike in the large cemetery located right in town—the pathways were wonderfully paved—and trading stuck-out tongues with the Sunday-dressed German kids. Old women, who greatly outnumbered any old men, all dressed in black, would shoo away us raggedy, whooping and playing Canadian kids.

The streets of Unna were not landscaped or affluent-looking then. All the buildings were stucco and the same beige or grey. No one had garages. We made friends with some German kids, but mostly stayed with our own kind in our own schools with our own commonality of base-kid lives. Again, it never occurred to me as a child that we were living in a foreign country. It was just where we lived.

L ife goes on. Germany would become a childhood memory. I treasure now that I was old enough to experience what I could, even what I didn't fully understand at ten years old.

Summer 1968: How to Get to Canada

Patriotism is bred into base kids. It makes sense; as children, we ourselves hadn't chosen to serve our country (yet) by joining up, but we felt like we had! And we didn't mind that feeling. We were proud of our pride.

The day my father came home from work in the spring of 1968 and replied to my mother's excited inquiry with the answer, "Goose Bay," was the start of another of our military family adventures.

"You're kidding me," she replied, or words to that effect.

"Get the Atlas," said Dad to our hopping questions.

I couldn't tell you if we had a Bible in the house, but we all knew where the Atlas was. I was ten years old, the big sister, with three younger brothers sprinkled in age down to three at the youngest. We'd been in Germany for two and a half years, living in our second house there, a nicely furnished military townhouse with bedrooms for all, and even a second bathroom. So, in the Army that meant time to move on for my sergeant father, and of course, for the rest of us with him.

"See, look here."

We shoved and crowded around Dad's finger pointing to the pink-coloured country displayed on the open pages.

"Goose Bay is in Canada. We're going home!" he exclaimed.

Home? I barely remembered moving to Germany from Calgary myself, and I'm sure my younger brothers didn't think of anywhere other than here in Unna as "home." My mother also rolled her eyes at the comment. She and my father were from Manitoba.

A few months later, there we all were, strapped in for landing on red lawn-chair style webbed seats in the Hercules C-130 aircraft on approach to Goose Bay, Labrador.

How the trip unfolded, however, was not as easy as all that. Given the circumstances, well, I can only marvel now at what must have been incredible stamina, organization, and downright clever problem-solving by the sergeant.

It started innocuously: a ride on the green army bus in pouring summer rain to Dusseldorf, to get on a gigantic propeller-driven airship called a Yukon. The flight was serene. I had my own seat away from brothers where I could read in peace, and the stewardess brought ice cold milk or any other drink at the lift of a finger. Parents were nowhere in sight, meaning all was well.

Arriving at CFB Trenton many, many hours later, we were all eager to shed our dressy, itchy travel clothes in the base hotel room overnight, to catch a train the next day to Montréal for an Air Canada flight to Goose Bay. That was the plan. Sitting with Mom while my wild brothers wrestled and played in the waiting room lobby, we watched Dad gesturing and pointing and slapping his hand down at the check-in counter. His uniform was probably even itchier than our clothes.

He returned with the news. "They weren't aware we were coming today."

No train tickets. They could get us on a late flight to Ottawa, and we could hitch a ride on a Hercules—a Herc—from there up to Goose Bay. My father disappeared again for a while, returning with box lunches, and told us we were having a picnic while we waited for our flight. Excellent! Box lunches were a special treat: sandwiches of soft pink meat, little milk or juice boxes and fruit and cookies and chocolate and gum. We loved them. The evening turned late, then in the dark, Dad collected us up and hustled us out over the tarmac up a little staircase where we ducked into an aircraft called a Dakota—a Dak. It only seated about twelve people and with us on it, it was full. We were the only family. The rest of the passengers wore all sorts of glittery uniforms, which meant officers, or "Brass," as my father would say, with that stern, pleading look that begged us to behave. Fortunately, my brothers were worn out enough to sleep on the short hop to Ottawa.

By arrival time in Ottawa, it had become pretty late, and we had an early flight the next morning, so why did my father insist the taxi take us downtown to find a hotel rather than stay out at the air base? I could ask him today, but I think I understand better now. He came from a small prairie town, son of immigrants. He and my mother had known each other since they were kids and had married young; they weren't even thirty years old yet at this time. He'd joined the Army at seventeen to escape the family farm life. He'd never been to Ottawa before, thousands of miles away from where he'd grown up. I figure he just wanted us to see Parliament Hill, because, by God, this was the chance. We were in the nation's capital!

It must have been two in the morning. Dad sat up front with the taxi driver while the rest of us squished into the back. How many hotels we drove up to, with my father still in uniform, running in, running out saying, "No room, no room"—I don't know. Finally, the taxi driver pulled up to the Lord Elgin but my father hesitated. The military would pay, but only so much, and it *was* the Lord Elgin. But, yes, they would take us. Well, not exactly a room.

"Kids, come on in!"

I don't know where my father and two brothers went, but my mother and I shared a closet-like space with two roll-out beds; she took one and my three year-old brother and I shared the other. I prayed he wouldn't wet the bed that night, but he probably did.

It didn't seem like more than a couple of hours later Dad was banging on our door.

"Come on, breakfast! Get dressed!"

We put our crumpled clothes back on and ate a fantastic bacon and eggs feast down in the fancy white-table-clothed dining room. Lots more Brass in sight. Were all the military in Ottawa officers? Sergeant Dad hurried us along.

Then out to the foreign streets of big-city Ottawa, excited and chattering as we hiked up to Parliament Hill. Rested and fed, my brothers ran up and back and around, my father pointing out statues and buildings that must have meant something or other. What did we know? We were *Kanadisher* kids, Canadian, yes, we'd been told; we'd been to the Canada Day parades in our German town, getting tank and horse rides for the occasion. But memories of our native land? I remembered the snow in Calgary. My latest home of Germany I recalled as always grey-green and wet. Now here today, in this our supposed "real" home of Canada, it was soft sunny blue and already comfortably warm at seven in the morning. My wool cape felt odd and heavy.

We arrived at the Hill, then stopped in awe, even my brothers. We'd had our share of European touring. My parents always insisted we visit castles and museums and war monuments—things like the Mohnesee Dam or the nearby Altena Castle. But nothing compared to that first sight of the red and white Canadian flag flying high above the Peace Tower. My father took a precious picture of us kids standing in front of the Eternal Flame, only a year old then, having been created for the Centennial the year before, which we'd celebrated patriotically as Canadians abroad. My father explained and espoused nonstop, our very own tour guide. We were mesmerized, like being inside a fairy tale, walking around that flame, nodding and listening to my father, identifying provincial flags in the stone, gawking like the transplanted aliens we still were. Early in the bright blue July morning, Canada was all ours, our own. My mother and father hugged; I think she cried a little showing us the bison on Manitoba's coat of arms.

"Welcome back to your own country, kids. You're Canadian, welcome home!"

Then the spell broke, and we were rushed into a taxi, out to the air base. Out across the tarmac again, in bright daytime now, we climbed up the back ramp of the Herc, and took turns after take-off on my father's shoulders to look out the port-hole window, too high up for sightseeing passengers.

A new chapter of our base-brat lives was about to begin. Goose Bay this time. Canada. Home.

*D*ad did tell me later that when the Herc landed in Goose Bay, the base commander was waiting with our family's sponsor, a military police sergeant, to properly greet him as the new Physical Education and Recreation Instructor (PERI) Sergeant to run the Base Recreation Centre. Goose Bay was an air base and my dad was Army. Dad said, as we got off the plane, he could hear the base commander say to the MP with him, "Oh shit, he's Army!"

I think the posting to Goose Bay had been some sort of punishment posting for a career misdeed of my dad's. I never did ask for details. As base kids, we didn't pay overmuch attention to our fathers' military careers. It was their job; we accepted whatever that meant for our own lives. That my father never got promoted past sergeant never registered as unusual to me. Lots of my friends' fathers were sergeants. Who cared?

1969-1970: "THE GOOSE" AND GOODBYES

*N**ow, for me, Goose Bay, Labrador was awesome, no matter what my parents thought of being banished to the frozen northern tundra. My grandmother had asked in a letter if they had houses for us or would we have to live in an igloo?*

I'm ten and eleven now, in grades five and six. I go to Goose Elementary and as an excellent student I soon earn my first place standing in class. Yes, in these times kids were ranked in order by their grades; pretty awful by today's reasoning, but as I was usually at the top of the class it never traumatized me. I was almost embarrassed by how easy some classes were, especially French. How could I not excel there? I'd been in the bilingual program in Germany at Werl DND and now the French teacher here with the Newfoundlander accent (no offence) was reciting how to count to ten and what the colours were. In later grades, I would go on to a Ukrainian-accented (again, no offence) French teacher in Saskatchewan. By the time I would get to high school in Petawawa with a real Francophone instructor, I would not be at the top of my French class, that's for sure! But here and now, I was a cocky, bright student with a new lifestyle to conquer.

Our school was mostly base kids, with the occasional Department of Transport (DOT) kid also attending, and even one or two civilian kids, like Peter, who seemed rich, but whose dad was probably only a manager or something at the Hudson's Bay store in Happy Valley. Even though my best friend Robin's dad was DOT, she lived in a PMQ down the street from me. Another best friend, Lori, lived a little farther down the hill in a separate area because her dad was an officer. I had a lot of friends in Goose Bay. It was that wonderful time: not a little kid anymore, but life hadn't yet become complicated. We still played outside all the time, which is saying a lot considering the weather. It was Labrador, northern Canada, after all.

We had a big ranch style PMQ, all furnished of course, because it was an isolated posting. I had my own bedroom as usual. Robin had an older sister she shared her room with. Her sister was beautiful and went to the base high school that was walking distance from the housing area. Robin thought she was a snob but I was in awe of her. Years later in Edmonton a corporal on my husband's hockey team revealed he was a base brat himself and had lived in Goose Bay, too. He'd dated Robin's sister. Such is the life!

We lived right on the runway. Actually, really, right on the runway. We could walk up to the pavement of one of the runways. There were some scrubby northern woods in between our house and the runway, but that was it. In these years there was a large American air base in Goose Bay, as well as a British air squadron. There were many, many runways. And sometimes in the middle of the night, I would be awakened—first, by the bright white lights strobing up the walls of my room, then by rumbling earthquake vibrations, followed by screeching roaring B-52 bombers tearing in line down the runway behind our house. Only to suddenly stop as each plane cut its engine in turn. This would repeat over and over. I don't know how many of these planes would be on this "Elephant Walk," which was what these Cold War practice alerts and take-offs (without actually taking off) were called. You'd think it would have been tiresome—they were always in the middle of the night—but I found them thrilling and was disappointed when the drill ended for the night.

My mother said you could tell first-year people in Goose Bay by whether or not they went outside—in the summer! Yes, the mosquitos and black flies were that terrible. But by the second summer you would suffer the bugs to get out; you'd been stuck indoors for so long during the brutal winter, the bugs didn't seem as bad as you'd thought that first year.

As kids, we didn't mind the winter or black fly season. We bundled up and after some frostbitten toes, my mother figured out we needed and therefore got sealskin boots from Hudson's Bay. I loved those boots. I had a fuzzy hat, too, which buttoned up under the chin, but I don't think it was sealskin. Thank goodness I was too young to know about Brigitte Bardot then. It wasn't like we had white *baby* sealskin anyway. We weren't rich.

We didn't think anything about the cold, but I do remember the coldest day of my life. Saturday mornings my father would take a couple of brothers to the arena on base for hockey. I would often go along, because of course it was a fun toboggan ride behind the skidoo. We always called the snowmobiles, or snow machines, by the brand name, *Skidoo*. As I said, we lived on the runway, and it was a shorter commute to the facilities part of the base from behind the PMQs on skidoo than to bother warming up the car and taking the roads the long way around. My dad drove the skidoo to work most days. It would always start. So this particular Saturday morning, we all wrapped up, my brothers dressed in hockey gear with big coats over it and boots on and our faces completely swaddled in scarves that my mother had knit, and settled in for the ride to the arena. When we got there, someone in the parking lot waved us over, and said hockey was cancelled because, didn't we know, it's 60 below out this morning! What were we thinking, coming in on the skidoo? Funny, I don't remember it being any colder or different feeling than usual. I guess after 30 or 40 or 50 below, what's another 10 degrees?

The woods out back and before the runways were our playground. In summer, forts and exploring. Gangs of kids meeting up, playing war or hide and seek. In winter we had skidoo riding, even driving. Yes, at eleven years old my parents let me take the skidoo on the weekends with my friends, when they roared up the front yard. There were no fences or signage or rules—just common sense and warm boots required. And stay away from the runways, of course. We used to think that the Americans patrolled and would shoot if you crossed over to their side. I don't think now that that was true. Even in sealskin, I froze my feet off. They still tingle and freeze easily today which is an after-effect of frostbite, I'm told, but boy, was it worth it.

Speaking of the Americans, they had the best stuff. Their base was miles and miles huge, their PX was way bigger than our CANEX stores, and they had a bigger movie theatre with a balcony. We could bus to their side and go to the Saturday matinees, where we would find exotic junk food like *Dr. Pepper* and *Butterfingers*. My mouth can still water remembering the melted chocolate on my fingers as I licked and sucked those golden buttery wonders of confection! *Dr. Pepper* was shockingly different from the coke or orange pop we had in our theatre, biting with that pleasing syrupy effervescence. I wouldn't get this stuff again after Goose Bay for decades.

The Saturday matinees were a big deal for us kids. We did have TV in Goose Bay, but it was a tiny black-and-white, one channel only, and nothing live. My father, a big Toronto Maple Leafs fan, would watch *Hockey Night in Canada* on two-week tape delays and act like he didn't know the results. Not that we kids didn't love our TV time anyway. These were the years of *Star Trek* and *The Monkees* and *Hawaii-Five O* (the original one). Great programming, even if it was only on one channel. My mother didn't mind the zombie-like quiet as we sat on the floor in the living room to watch TV. One channel only meant no squabbling about it.

The moon landing happened when we were in Goose Bay. July 20, 1969. Of course we didn't watch it live on TV, but I remember it vividly. On such a pure-black cloudless night in Labrador, the moon was brilliant. Although only in waxing crescent phase that night, we could still see the outline of the whole moon against its fluorescent quarter. As my mother gathered us in the backyard to look, my brothers and I imagined the men walking on it at that exact moment. We jumped up and down exclaiming we could see them. Over the many times later in life when watching the grainy black-and-white film footage of that historic moment, I would always think of us, my mother and brothers and me, in our dark sandy backyard, lights out, looking up to the heavens to watch the moon landing, live.

Like all fairy tales, Goose Bay ended much too soon for me. We'd only been there two years when my father announced in the spring that we were posted "home" that summer to the Prairies—to Yorkton, Saskatchewan. He and my mother were from small-town Manitoba, so I guess I understand now why they were excited. We'd been in Germany before Goose Bay for almost three years; they hadn't seen their parents or siblings in five years. But for me, this news felt uncomfortable and I didn't understand why. I knew we were military, and would have to move eventually. Everyone did. Confused, I felt the last days before school letting out were speeding by much too quickly.

I turned twelve that spring and our softball team hadn't won a game yet. The coaches had promised us a barbeque if we ever won. That didn't seem likely; we were the only Canadian team in the league and those American girls could sure play ball. I was hanging out after swimming in the pool change room with Robin when I said I wasn't going to bother to go to the softball game that night. We sucked so bad and what did it matter—I was moving and wouldn't finish the season anyway. Maybe teenage angst was beginning. I didn't recognize the depression setting in over leaving that upcoming summer. But Robin was insistent. She promised that even if we didn't win, she was sure we were going to have a barbeque. And then she told me something that to this day I regret forcing out of her.

"We're having a surprise going-away party for you after the game. And you can't tell anyone I told you!"

Well, what can I say now?

We played as usual that night, so we lost, as usual. But the coach did shuttle us all to his backyard in the back of his pickup truck, where a big hot dog barbeque with pop awaited. I was eating and sitting in a circle with all my friends, when the coach asked for attention and announced my going-away. He made a little speech, mentioning my great glove at first base, thanking me and wishing me luck on my move to Yorkton. Then he handed me a card, all signed by the team, and a wrapped present. Completely choked up into a silence no one thought me capable of, I numbly unwrapped the gift. A ceramic horse. I collected them.

I finally realized I was going to have to say goodbye to Goose Bay. To my ball team. To my friends. At twelve years old, I didn't recognize this feeling yet, this ache and hurt. But over the years of moving, and as life did get complicated, it would become familiar, and always dreaded. Saying goodbye was the duty I tried hard to accept, not always with success. There were times I avoided making new friends in anticipation of those horrible goodbyes. I know now they were growing experiences, enriching and making precious every acquaintance of life, but at twelve years old, it was a new and painful lesson.

*A*lthough we never kept in touch, I remember and thank *you, Robin, and Lori, and Goose Bay.*

REFLECTIONS OF CHILDHOOD

*A*s I write these stories, of course I want to highlight the fun and interesting aspects of growing up and living the military lifestyle. But it was not a perfect life, and not even a most desirable one. Many of us who grew up like this carry the scarred baggage of the multiple moves and unnatural living conditions. Our lives weren't like those of the rest of society. It was a parallel universe, things seemingly similar with the outside world, but somehow slightly off, different. If we lived near a civilian community, it was always us versus them, as in base kids versus townies, and it was rare to mix. Why should we? We had our own self-contained community, complete with recreation facilities: pool, gym, bowling alley, hockey rink—all for free or near enough. Our own schools, complete with our own school buses, if necessary. Our own grocery and other stores, like Maple Leaf Services or Canex. Our own churches. Our own libraries. Safe streets. Ready-made communities. The first thing we did upon arrival at a new PMQ was check out the layout of our new base, but no matter the size of it, from the tiny radar station in Yorkton to the large base of Petawawa, all the pieces of a ready-made life were in place. Just the scale, geography, and weather were different.

We usually lived far from relatives. I remember Christmas and Thanksgiving in Germany, spent with my father's cousin's family because he was in the Army over there, too. He was the closest relative I remember from childhood. I thought he was my uncle. My parents, understandably homesick for family and hometown—they themselves didn't grow up military—always included a side trip on our posting travel for extended visits to the small prairie towns of their childhood where their own siblings and parents still lived their farming and associated lives. It might as well have been Mars to me. A cousin I met when I was twelve told me she envied my life of moving around, seeing the world. I didn't understand what she meant; I couldn't imagine being stuck in the same town, the same house for my whole life. At twelve, I could already count seven homes I had lived in. I was amazed that at thirteen, she had painted her own bedroom. I'd never even seen that done. All the houses we'd moved into were freshly painted that basic industrial white. The only variation was that in a year you could see the yellowed nicotine stains above any armchair my father sat in. At moving time, we would have to be "marched out," that is, the house had to be inspected. My mother would start the intensive cleaning a week in advance, one room at a time, and keep that room off limits to us kids once it was done. By march-out, we would have been stuck sitting on the step outside for the last day or so. It wasn't a hardship; it was the way our world worked. You did what you were told and didn't complain.

Ah, then the move. When we weren't flying across the Atlantic or back, it was a road trip, and our holiday. We never went to Disneyland or anything, just visited the relatives on our way across the country. Motels with beds you put quarters in to vibrate (all the better for jumping on). Outdoor pools. We always moved in the summer, right after school let out. Restaurant meals even for breakfast, which was wonderful as it was a treat in those days to eat out. Chasing down the escaped family dog in a strange town. One time visiting my grandfather in Carberry, Manitoba our beloved pet—his name was Cognac, yes, for the booze, (his mother's name was Brandy and my parents named him, despite saying he was *my* eleventh birthday present)—well, Cognac went nuts barking at and chasing kids on horseback. On horseback on the town streets! We couldn't catch the darn dog and were lucky the horses didn't buck or bolt. Well, not too much. Another time we had to banish Cognac to the car and leave Great Auntie's place in Holmfield, Manitoba a little early after he "allegedly" killed one of her backyard chickens. The new prairie life of our beloved Cognac must have been just as bewildering to a puppy born in Labrador as it was for the rest of us, having lived all our childhoods so far in Germany and Goose Bay. My parents of course loved going home. My brothers and I never knew what that felt like. So far, we'd only left homes; we'd never gone back to any.

There were consequences to being raised in such a life. Many of them positive. We experienced a variety in our lives of geography, weather, people, and cultures. But other consequences had not been so good. With no input or heads-up, every couple of years—two? three?—we'd be ripped from our familiar: our homes, our friends, our progression of life. When I left Goose Bay I was twelve, yet already anticipating the following year there when I would have been promoted at my Sunday School to assistant teacher. By leaving when I did, I missed that opportunity. Not a big deal in the scheme of things, but the first adult-like regret of missing out on something I'd worked to set up. It left an impression. We either grew up too fast to keep up, or we stalled too long and played catch-up later.

Of course, the moving on, the excitement, the anticipation! This was the best part of growing up military. What would the next place be like?

Adolescence and a new life awaited, and I would be too old to go to Sunday school there. On to Yorkton, Saskatchewan.

PART TWO. TURBULENT TEENS.

1970-1973: CFS YORKTON, SASKATCHEWAN

Whatever had caused my father to be "punishment-posted" to Goose Bay obviously wasn't over yet. Next move was to a tiny radar station—another Air Force posting—out west, in the middle of the Saskatchewan prairie, called Canadian Forces Station (CFS) Yorkton. Maybe not punishment for my parents because it was driving distance to their relatives and their own home town; it might even have been a reward posting for doing two tours in a row so far from home. But it felt like punishment for me, at first. CFS Yorkton was too small to be called CFB, for Base. And it wasn't in the city of Yorkton, but about ten kilometers away, at the turnoff for the grain elevators that were emblazoned with the town name of Orcadia under the larger POOL sign. Having western parents, I knew this word was the term for the farmers' cooperative to pool their grain for shipment, but my mother told me about a young Maritimer wife who, upon arrival in the prairies, casually mentioned that "My goodness, they sure have a lot of high-diving boards in their pools out here!"

After the elevators and over the railroad tracks, you still had a few more kilometers down that gritty unpaved road, with farm fields to either side, past the low ditches, to get to the gate of the base. Imagine wheat fields encircling the horizon, with a quarter-section carved out squarely in the middle, where low bland military buildings and trailer-park PMQs were plunked in organized Legoland-like configurations. Nothing over two storeys high, and wide clear sky above. Then there were the radar domes themselves, "up the hill." CF-Yorkton station was part of NORAD's Pinetree line. Like the DEW line, it was a part of a string of radar bases set up as Distant Early Warning stations. Cold War stuff. There was not much of a hill on that flat, open-plained land. More like a slight rise. The domes looked like giant golf balls, white and dimpled, and showed for kilometers away over the wheat-rippled horizon.

A couple of radar domes don't require a huge military contingent to operate. There were only about 90 PMQs at CFS Yorkton, and our school on base included all grades from kindergarten to grade eight. There were ten of us in grade seven and the following year I was the only girl in my grade eight class of five. The school had no gym. We'd go once a week to the base Rec Centre, where my father was the ranking boss, still as sergeant, to play on the trampoline or go bowling or play dodgeball or badminton. All equipment was available and, of course, all for free. There was a swimming pool, if only outdoors. The Rec Centre became the center of our teenage world every day after supper. The gym was open for sports every night and was in a single-building complex that included a small grocery store, a little restaurant where we'd buy French fries, and even a library, where my mother would eventually work. Across the road was the multi-denominational church, whose common room was also designated our "Teen Town" in the evenings and on weekend days. We'd get movies on Friday nights, even the R-rated ones, because who would stop us? The base was its own jurisdiction and as long as the commanding officer said it was okay, it was. We'd play cards and records every other time. On such a small base, all the teenagers ranging in age from thirteen on up hung out together; there weren't enough of us not to!

Another Beginning

The following story is how I remember arriving at Yorkton and moving in. Unique to base kids, we all understood and expected that new kids would come, others would go. Thanks to our shared sufferance of the moving whims of the military, there was an unspoken code of conduct. I don't remember any bullying of new kids like I've heard about in civilian life—on "civvie street," as we called it. Not yet, that is. In high school I would be offered a different greeting upon arrival, but that's for later! This story shows how important the sense of base-kid community was to me, at an important time in my life. It was the start of growing up.

Her mother practically pushed her out the door of their new PMQ when the girls showed up.

"Mickey, get out here. Some girls are calling on you!" her mother shouted.

"Who? I don't know anyone!" Mickey hollered back from her room. She was reading and didn't appreciate the interruption. The PMQ was just a double-wide mobile home, and the walls were easy enough to yell through. Mickey had heard the tinny knocks on the aluminum screen door, open to the oven-like prairie heat of the late summer day. *How could there be any girls here for me?* she wondered.

They'd just moved in a couple of days earlier. Mom still had boxes in the living room to unpack while they waited for furniture to buy. Coming from the isolated postings of Goose Bay and Germany before this one to Yorkton, where everything had been provided, her family didn't have any relevant furniture. Mickey had a mattress on the floor of her room. Her own room, at least. The room that she left now to see who was at the door.

"My name is Sharon and this is Barbara," said the girl on the step with the long blond pony-tail, to Mickey's mother. Mickey walked up behind to peek out.

"We're two of the total of four—now five—girls that are going into grade seven. We hear there's a grade-seven girl moving in here, right?" Sharon, hair flipping around her tanned cheeks and bubbly blue eyes bright, now peered around to see Mickey come to the door.

"That's true! How nice of you girls! Mickey, go out with these nice girls. Go play!"

How embarrassing. But as her mother had physically pushed Mickey out in front, there was no choice but to step outside.

They walked along, Sharon chattering away, oblivious to the shimmering heat rising above the asphalt of the narrow road that meandered around the PMQ area. It was so hot! No breeze at all. No trees for shade. Everything was dusty pale—dry sage-coloured lawns, the wide sky a bleached wash of blue on this quiet August workday mid-afternoon. Barbara trailed a little behind, content to let Sharon point out houses and fill in gossip about who lived where, as they ambled by. Barbara was short with freckles and a bob of strawberry blond hair. Pretty buxom already at twelve, Mickey noticed, feeling bewildered. Scrawny with straight long brown hair, Mickey wasn't even in a training bra yet. Who were these kids and where were they taking her? She hadn't explored the base much yet.

She needn't have worried. Although all the trailer PMQs looked alike, low and dirty white with warbled plastic yellowish carports in front, they had prominent numbers that went down in sequence quite visibly. There was only one road with a loop near the end; it wouldn't be hard to get home, or take very long. Sharon stopped at one marked about number 25, and said, "I live here, come on in."

By "in" she meant under the attached carport, where a few other young teenagers were sitting in lawn chairs or otherwise hanging out in the shade of the afternoon. A record player was perched on the concrete step, plugged into the outdoor outlet meant for a car block heater. Mickey couldn't imagine a winter cold enough here in what looked to her like a desert landscape. It was nothing like the stunted conifers and rocky tundra she'd left in Labrador. At least she was already tanned from the visits to relatives in Manitoba along the road trip here. She'd never noticed before in Germany and Goose Bay whether she tanned or not.

Now she noticed something else: a cute dark-haired boy who was looking at record albums as the girls walked in. He jumped up as Sharon introduced Mickey to the group, sputtering something about a baseball game or albums he liked or something. Mickey didn't register what he was saying exactly, distracted by the loose bangs hanging over his eyes.

She browsed the albums for a while. The Beatles, Creedence Clearwater Revival, The Doors. Sharon must have older siblings by the looks of this "mature" collection. Mickey herself was a fan of the Monkees. She liked Peter, probably just to be different, since Davy Jones was the acknowledged heartthrob.

"Do you play ball?" Doug, the cute boy, asked.

"Ball? Softball? Yes, sure." Of course she did!

"We go to the school field most nights after supper. Bring your glove."

"Do you like Bobby Sherman?" asked Sharon.

Sharon put on the 45. Well, Mickey had just moved in from Goose Bay, not Mars. She read *Tiger Beat*; of course she liked Bobby Sherman!

Maybe this new weird base wasn't going to be so bad after all, she thought, humming along with *Julie Do Ya Love Me*.

And it wasn't.

*M*usic—*soother of the teenage beast. If I had to give a one-word answer to describe the most important part of early teenage years, it would be music.*

We listened to everything. The older teenagers controlled the record player at Teen Town, so they would play whole albums of the Beatles, Bob Dylan, The Moody Blues. I loved songs like Sugar Mountain *by Neil Young, which was only the B-side to* Heart of Gold, *and which the local AM radio station would never have played.*

I myself taped my own collection from the TV or radio. I'd bully my brothers to silence while the Partridge Family was on so I could sit close and put the wired mike from my cassette recorder up to the TV speaker to get David Cassidy loud and clear. My favourite song on the radio in those days was Guitar Man by Bread. I also loved Magic Carpet Ride by Steppenwolf, Long Cool Woman by the Hollies, and Bang-a-Gong by T-Rex. And American Pie, of course. I could (probably still can) recite from memory every line of that multi-verse song.

I still had my old Monkees albums, but didn't listen to them as much anymore. I was buying Alice Cooper (to drive my parents crazy over that Billion Dollar Baby cover) and Deep Purple. But mostly I became a lover of the collections; K-Tel started with their anthology albums in those days. I was—still am—a radio lover and a puncher of buttons to station-switch. In Yorkton, on clear prairie nights, you could tune into American stations from places as far away as Chicago and St. Louis. Only at night, though.

I had plenty of nights to listen, as these were also the baby-sitting-for-money years. Fifty cents an hour, and more after midnight, if the people were generous. The one and only TV station went off the air around midnight when what was known as the Indian head test screen appeared. So, after that I'd play the family's albums: The Beatles Sgt. Pepper's Lonely Hearts Club Band, The Osmonds, the Jackson Five, Three-Dog Night, and Neil Diamond. If the family didn't own anything good, I could always play the radio and even phone in for requests. April Wine was popular. I even saw them in concert back then.

Of course, all this music wasn't wasted on just listening. We had dances at Teen Town at least once a month, and kids did dance in those days, even the boys. We dressed up for special dances, like Easter or Sadie Hawkins, where the girls got to invite a boy to be her date for the night. At Christmas, the base would let us use their lounge at the all-ranks mess for a fancier affair. My mother reworked a dress that she'd made for my Anglican confirmation the year before; it was white crepe with long bell sleeves and an empire waist, so she added a gold filigree band. I looked and felt like an angel. I even let her curl my hair for the event, something I wouldn't do again until the eighties, when everyone with straight hair had to get permed for most of that fluffy decade.

I still love music, and not just the oldies. I like my music new and varied, like life. Hard to attribute my diverse taste in music to being a base brat, but I do think the craving for variety comes from getting around. No matter either way!

THE LAST DRESS

*C*aution: *Teenage girl. No crossing.*

Her mother must have felt like crying as she watched her twelve-year-old daughter take the large pinking shears to the beautiful blue organza dress, a hand-me-down given by a neighbour for the teen dance that evening.

"I hate dresses!" Mickey had screamed, "I want a new top for my jeans tonight, or I'm not going!"

Mickey had always been a headstrong girl—bright, independent, stubborn. Very stubborn. But that fall, along with puberty, had been especially terrible; they'd moved from Goose Bay to Yorkton, Saskatchewan that past summer. Friends had been replaced, there was a new school on a new base—a new country, more like—to negotiate. Even language differences, going by some early teasing of her "Newfie" accent. She'd quickly learned to drawl like a local.

Sighing, her mother had gently taken the sewing scissors from her. "Michele, let me help. You'll cut it too high." And she not only helped, but as usual, she finished it for her eldest, her only daughter, who Mom never seemed to tire of trying to reason with.

Mickey's eyes watered with frustration. Why was she

always so angry with her mother, anyway? And why couldn't her mother see how ugly and old-fashioned the stupid dress was?

"Get out of here!" Mickey screamed as a wayward brother poked his head around the corner, on his way through the tiny living room to scoot out the back door in the kitchen. "We're busy! You boys are always in the way!"

Brothers, hand-me-downs, first teenage dances. Years later it was obvious to Michele what was going on in her life in those days.

That lovely filmy dress, made into a top those decades ago, had certainly never been her style, but her mother, pins in mouth, had cut and hemmed and carefully chosen and sewn new buttons on it, listening and nodding all the while to her daughter's rants about the sucky colour, the horrible style—without a word of complaint. And although she'd worn it to the dance, Mickey had thrown that top out in the garbage the next day.

*W*hat can I say? My poor mother. I think she was glad I was the only girl she had!

I wonder today how much the moves at such a time of life contributed to such teenage angst? What difference does it make? Having raised two teenagers now myself, I know that everyone, child and parent alike, muddles through whatever adolescence they are dealt.

What was interesting to the teenage mind I was learning to navigate then was the blossoming realization that there were so many different places available in the world, each with its own culture and artifacts: from northern sealskin boots and skidooing, to learning how to curl on the Prairies by sticking duct tape on your sliding foot. I would go from school topics about iron-ore mining in geography and hydro-electric politics in Newfoundland, to learning the history of Doukhobor farming immigrants, and what a section was in Saskatchewan. Although I didn't even know the word, I thought I'd invented the idea of anthropology at thirteen, because I was living it. I would enjoy the observation of the "natives" until I became one. And then move on to the next case study.

I also noted that the base kids everywhere were mostly the same, as if we were transported around together in a spaceship, to land on another different planet, like from Arctic tundra to desert prairie. Although the same in yet indefinable ways, we base kids couldn't help but absorb the locale around us. Every place left its touch.

Have you heard that scientists can tell by your tooth enamel where in the world you grew up? It's done by detecting the unique isotope signatures of some element or another that are absorbed in developing teeth from the local water. I'd love to see the confusion of the scientist studying my tooth enamel. From birth to age twelve, my tooth-building years occurred in the diverse locations of Calgary, Alberta; Kingston, Ontario; back to Calgary; Northern Germany; Goose Bay, Labrador, and then to Yorkton, Saskatchewan. I'm sure my isotopes are quite the mixture. Maybe their signature matches some place I've never even been to? Or maybe each tooth grew at a different time and so was different from its neighbour? I guess that's why when statistics are quoted, the lesson is to pay attention to the degree of confidence and the margins of error. There are exceptions to all the rules. Just sayin'!

Dr. Brass Junior High School

The first real civilian school I ever attended was Dr. Brass Junior High School, in town, in the city of Yorkton, Saskatchewan. It was a big school, with about four or five classes of about thirty kids for each grade of seven, eight, and nine. It still had a dress code, which in 1972 was becoming old-fashioned, as the hippies of the sixties started to become our teachers. Not yet, though, here at Dr. Brass. We couldn't wear jeans, which had become my daily uniform the previous year in grade eight. It was bewildering, and I couldn't stand dresses!

Although I had always been a good student, the townie kids in grade nine had had two previous years of courses in things like music, home economics, art, and physical education. All the fun stuff, but for me, my worst marks. I passed them all, though, through luck, bluffing, and not exactly cheating, but improvising. For example, I passed music by getting my friend Patti to write my assignment song. *Write a song? I can't read or write music!* But I had Patti write the notes out as I plunked them on her mother's piano. And for my passing mark of D in Phys Ed—*A test on Basketball rules? Volleyball? You're kidding—* at least I was able to do flips on the trampoline for the gymnastics test; we played on the tramp' all the time back in the Rec Centre on base.

And don't get me started about Home Economics! It was so sexist I couldn't help but rebel in this class. As mentioned, we weren't allowed to wear jeans at Dr. Brass, but of course I always wore pants—slacks they were called—of some sort. But on Home Ec days, which, by the way, were only for girls (I did say sexist, right?), we were instructed to wear dresses to school! Unbelievable, except even worse, the boys on those days had Shop classes (also sexist), and get this, they were permitted to wear jeans to Shop! After a couple of these days getting incredibly teased by my base-boy friends with things like, "Haha! Sucker! In a dress while we get to wear jeans!" or some variation of this, well, one day I just wore my jeans on Home Ec day. The other girls gasped in shock. The teacher didn't say a word. And although I picked up the sewing and other girl-required skills well enough to get good grades on my assignments, I did receive a D in Home Economics also. Which I accepted with pride. In fact, society finally moving on even at Dr. Brass, at the end of the year the teachers offered a trial whereby volunteer girls could take a shop class or two if they wanted. I of course did so, and made a beautiful silver ring by learning and using the lost-wax method.

I still have that ring.

THE GANG AND THE SNOWSTORM

*H*ere's *a little story about heading into the city for one of those grade nine days.*

Michele ran out the door into the blowing snow. *Does it ever just snow straight down?* she wondered, clutching her hood tight to her face as the stinging crystals were slung sideways into her eyes by the ever-constant prairie wind. She'd waited inside breathing and scratching frosty designs on the window of the screen door until she saw the dark green shape of the school bus coming around the corner. The bus stopped in front of her PMQ and she slogged through the drift on the edge of the road to step up and onboard. The young corporal designated as the bus driver today slammed the door shut behind her and moved along. How he could tell where the road was, Michele couldn't imagine—the drifts and blowing snow swirled into whiteout in every direction.

But that wasn't her problem. She moved towards the middle of the bus, nearer the front, actually. The back was reserved for the high school kids. As a first year rider into the city for grade nine, she knew better than to take a seat too far back. No one talked much in the mornings, and the other kids seemed especially quiet today, cocooned as they were from the storm inside their protective army bus shell.

The highway was even more desolate than usual on the ten-kilometer drive to the city of Yorkton. The black top of the asphalt sifted in and out of existence with the whirls of white snow chasing across it. It looked like white-tipped ocean waves undulating across the road. Everyone dozed, hypnotized.

The bus slowed on arrival to the city and the traffic lights. Michele and the other junior high students—there were only five of them today out of the normal nine, and Debbie, the only other girl in grade nine from the base, was one of the no-shows—wiggled to life, adjusting scarves and hoods as they prepared to get out at Dr. Brass Junior High. The bus stopped there first before heading off with the older kids to the city high school. The lone girl again today, Michele was quite used to it. Only one of the boys in the group was in her class anyway. There were four grade nine classes in Dr. Brass, Class A, which she and Wayne were in, and then a B, C, and D class. Yes, the class name corresponded to the academic expectations of their students. Ridiculous, but such was the streaming process of the times.

"Pretty shitty out here. Let's see if we can get inside the lobby this morning," Steve shouted over the wind. He usually took the lead and was sixteen, two years older than the rest of them, so obviously in Class D. Michele didn't trust him much, and didn't hang out with him and his older crowd on base, but of course went along with his leadership here at school. She didn't mind that his tough reputation kept other townie cliques from being too aggressive with the base kids. They stuck together in town.

So with the others, she clutched her paper lunch bag and shuffled up the concrete stairs in the blowing snow to the front doors of the school.

"They're locked!" Terry shouted.

Steve tried them anyway. Then they all peered into the windows of the doors and Steve started to bang on the glass. Yes, they usually had to wait outside before class but the doors were never locked. What was the problem today?

"School's closed," Wayne suggested. "There is a storm, you know."

Steve punched him in the arm, and Wayne moved off to the side.

Then a janitor came and opened the door for the huddled group. "No school today. Go home," he said with a heavy Ukrainian accent.

"We're the base kids. Our bus is gone. We can't go home. Let us in!"

The older man paused, and Steve barged his way in, the rest of them following. Michele stopped to thank the janitor while the boys trooped in, and said they wouldn't stay long; they just needed to warm up. Backing away, he said, "Okay, but just stay here, in lobby. Half-hour only. Then go home."

The boys were stamping their feet and moving to sit on the stairs leading up to the main floor of the school. Michele stood back a bit. What were they supposed to do now? The base bus wouldn't be back until 3:00 p.m. or so. It wasn't even nine yet.

In the meantime, someone opened their lunch and

started eating a sandwich. Michele joined him. She was always hungry, even though she'd had some oatmeal already that morning. The ham and cheese tasted especially good and salty today, as it would after the biting cold outside. *We have to think of something to do about being stranded for the day in the snowstorm*, she thought, chewing the pasty white bread.

Alan's mother worked at the Eaton's department store downtown. Some of the kids would get rides home from her if they wanted to hang out after school, and if she was working late that day.

"She only works until one today, but the car can't take us all," Alan said when Michele asked if they could go downtown and get a ride home with her. It was a plan anyway, so they decided to head there. At least Alan's mom could phone someone for them.

They hung out a little longer. Everyone had decided to eat their lunch by now. Then the janitor came back, and started mopping up the mess their boots had melted into on the marble floor.

Steve got up and so they all did up their heavy coats and put on mitts and raised hoods and headed back out into the whirling whiteness of the day.

Tramping together down the city streets, boys pushing and wrestling each other along the way, they got to the big Eaton's store, which would be their shelter for the day. Alan's mother promised them a ride at one. They dallied around to browse. Clerks followed them, giving warning looks, so they split up and wandered the varied departments. Michele found the jewellery counter and took a lot of time dawdling and peering into glass countertops, but the lady working didn't offer any help. She tried on clothes, picking out tops that she could save up to buy with babysitting money. The boys went to the electronics area to sit on furniture and look at the console TV sets, until a salesman would shoo them away, but they'd go right back after he left. Finally the group met up at the store cafeteria early for lunch—a couple of the guys could be depended on to have enough money to buy a plate of fries or two to split. They squished in together at a booth. After downing her water, Michele dumped coffee cream from the round glass jug on the table into her now empty glass to drink when the waitress left. Thick and rich, with the added sugar poured in, it was like warm, melted ice cream. Delicious. They ate and dawdled, the four of them. Steve had disappeared sometime in the morning to find his own way home. No one kept tabs on him.

Alan's mom drove the rest of them back to the base, snow still snaking sideways on the highway like ethereal creatures whipping in and out of existence, but there was not much new accumulation, just the ever-present living wind. They all got out at Alan's PMQ and made their way back to their own places.

"Mom? I'm home. School was cancelled today. I'm starving!" Michele hollered.

"What? What did you do all day then?"

"Nothing," she replied. "What's for supper?"

*B*ase *kids were like any kids—each different, and not all friends with everyone, but as a group, we understood our bond, and when in trouble or in town, we stuck together. I can see why the townies thought of us as a gang. It was a reputation we encouraged, because people, especially*

teenagers, are sensitive to people who are "other," that is, not of the town. Base kids were not "of the town." We were always "other."

Even the civilian teachers treated us as a separate group—cohesive—despite the nine of us being distributed in different classes. I remember a Friday afternoon school dance with lights dimmed and a DJ set up on the stage in the gym. Girls lined up along one wall and boys on the other. Except for us base kids. We'd find each other and stand together: Debbie and I, and the boys, a few of whom had city girlfriends—groupie-like it seems to me now, like hangers-on. A teacher I didn't know came right up to me and asked me to please get the base boys to go and ask girls to dance, as in, "Could you base kids please get the dance started?" It was a surprising moment for me—a teenage girl suddenly required to act in a mature leadership role. I guess we were more mature about some things. And of course, we did get the dance started.

I never thought about it until years later, but, why did our bus take us to school in a snowstorm? Because the corporal driver was told to drive the bus. Because we were told to go to school. Because we were base kids, tough and smart, able to deal with what we were dealt. That's my answer! It helps explain to me why we seemed more mature sometimes.

RECALLED

*O*ne time:

Me: What was it like, Mom, having four kids by the time you were 26?

Mom: I don't know. Diapers, babies . . . I don't remember much about my 20s!

Me: What about your 30s?

Mom: God, you were all teenagers. Those were the years I drank!

*A*nother time:

Me: Mom, how come you had four kids? And why did you stop after four?

Mom: Well, your baby brother was born in 1965. The same year all my friends had their last kid.

Me: Really? All your friends had their last baby in 1965?

Mom: 1965 was the year we got the Pill.

1973: YORKTON TO PETAWAWA, ONTARIO

*F*riends *come and go.*

Sharon and Barbara moved away after grade seven.

In grade eight, my best friend became Patti. She was a year younger in grade seven. Her mom played the organ and ran the church choir, so I joined the choir. I loved singing.

I had a boyfriend in grade eight. He was in grade seven, but my age.

My boyfriend moved away after grade eight.

Patti moved away in March of my grade nine year. She was still going to school on base while I was bused to the city.

I didn't have a boyfriend in grade nine; I just enjoyed the dances with all of them.

After grade nine we moved away. To Petawawa.

*A*s physically different as Yorkton had been from Goose Bay, so was Petawawa from Yorkton. My father had finally been posted back to the Army, and boy, was CFB Petawawa a real army base. As big as a small city, even bigger than the small civilian town of Petawawa outside the gates, the PMQs were so numerous they were even divided into two sites, one north and one south of the Petawawa River. It was home to, among others at that time, a big artillery unit. My future boyfriend/husband's father was the artillery regimental sergeant major (RSM) stationed there. This was considered a high position in the community and so my parents were impressed when I started dating Don. It was almost as good as dating an officer's son. I myself though, like most of the other base kids, didn't attach much importance to my father's rank. I can't remember many times when it mattered. I do remember lifeguarding with the daughter of the base commander—Highest of the High. It seemed to impress our parents more than us kids.

We could hear the big guns out on the ranges from the PMQs. Like the planes in Goose Bay, we soon got used to the thunderous subtext to the day.

It was ruggedly beautiful in Petawawa. The PMQs on the south side where we lived were enshrouded by tall pine trees in those days. I've returned there since, and most of those trees are gone, but back then, my mother was horrified by them. It was like being in the forest and she, ever the prairie girl, hated them. She missed the sky.

As kids, though, we enjoyed the woods, and the rocks, and the river. Like in Goose Bay, the woods became our playground, which for teenagers meant our hang-out spot for parties. And the river, ah, the beautiful, deadly, tempting Petawawa River! It didn't take my brothers and I long to find the paths through the woods, up and down hills, and scramble over rocks large enough to sprawl on, to the rapids where natural waterslides, waves, currents, and swirly pools awaited. We were all good swimmers, but that wasn't the prerequisite for playing there; a teenage hunger for thrills was all that was required. And

I certainly had that. Those rapids were wonderful on the fading muggy Ontario days of summer. You had to wear cutoff shorts for the sliding or you'd tear the ass out of your bathing suit on those rocks. Fun times!

But the summer of moving was finally over; the first day of school—high school this time—awaited.

1973: LAZY DAYS OF SUMMER. HAZING DAYS OF SCHOOL.

I think it was my mother who was partly responsible for the end of the hazing initiation rituals at General Panet High School that fall of 1973. I will never be able to prove it—Mom is gone now, and Dad wasn't involved. But this is the story of why I think what I think.

Finally, school was starting today. I never minded the end of summer holidays. By late August, I'm always ready to go back. Especially this year, after the long summer of moving, with all the family visits and awkward hangouts with strange cousins in their confusing prairie farm towns. I'd had enough of cramped backseat car rides with brothers fighting to sit by the window. I always got a window, of course, where I could read and escape the mayhem.

Finally, another first day—this one of high school—in Petawawa, Ontario.

Schools in Canada are all run provincially, and this caused some inconsistencies transferring to a new system when we moved. Ontario was the only province that had thirteen grades. Because we'd just come from

Saskatchewan, I was bumped up a grade to eleven, skipping ten. I was allowed to take one grade ten course, in Biology, because I was interested and insisted, but it turns out I would get 100% in that class. In fact, it was a repeat of everything they'd taught in grade nine General Science at Dr. Brass in Yorkton. I remember an extremely kind Mr. Lariviere saying to me as I waited for him to mark my lab notebook, "I don't normally give a mark of 100%, but why not? You've earned it." I didn't know then that he was dying of cancer, and probably already knew it when he gave me that mark. Thank you, sir!

But that was later in the year. Back to that first week in General Panet. If I'd thought Dr. Brass had been an adjustment from grade school to junior high, with its four or five classes each of grades seven, eight, and nine, I was blown away by this metropolis of a high school. It had grades nine to thirteen, two gyms, a football field, wood and metal and plastics shops, and home economics' kitchens. There was a large parking lot area for the school buses. Extra portable trailer classrooms stood in place—after all, we were the peak of the baby-boomer generation hitting these years. There was even a smoking area for students. This was the seventies; everyone smoked. Not me, though. I hated cigarettes. At least smoking wasn't allowed inside the school.

I was sitting in class when the announcement came over the PA system. Still shy with my new teenage classmates all a year older than me, the boys looked like men, broad-shouldered and tall, and the girls like young women wearing tight jeans, tank tops, and eyeliner. Although fifteen myself now, I was still skinny and of course wore no makeup; I could probably still pass for twelve. This day

I was wearing my Molson Ukrainian T-shirt with Lee jeans and North Star runners.

"All new students, please report to the gym."

The teacher pointed at me and a few others, and we obediently left class.

No teachers greeted us at the gym. I was ushered up steps to the hardwood stage by older students, to stand confused with other kids behind the heavy velvet curtains in the wings. It was hot and musty and I started to sweat. What was going on?

There was to be an auction, someone said. A slave auction. Senior students would buy one of us freshmen to act as that senior's slave for the rest of the first week of school. Talk about landing on another planet—I had never even heard of hazing before!

I didn't make it onto the stage in front of the buyers. An older boy in grade thirteen, who was really a young man of eighteen, grabbed my arm. He wasn't tall and had bad skin. Like everyone, he wore jeans and a tight-fitting T-shirt, and had ragged sideburns to match an unruly tangle of longish hair.

"I guess I'll take you," he said. "I wanted a boy but you look like the next best thing since they're all gone."

I had no idea what he was talking about.

"Stay here," he added. "I'll be back with my instructions."

Now, no one who's ever known me would disagree if I said I'd always been somewhat rebellious. I question authority and demand answers; I talk back if I think I should. Even as a young girl, I was a "women's libber" before I knew what that was. As older sister to three brothers, I had always insisted on equality and expected it. So, what did I do that day on the auditorium stage in the gym at General Panet High School?

I waited for my "master," Kevin, to return to give me my instructions as his slave for the week.

No, I can't explain why, but I guess I just couldn't believe what was going on.

Instructions given, the next day I wore my jeans inside out, painted freckles on my face, and tied my hair into three pigtails. My mother smiled, my brothers didn't dare make fun, and off to the bus stop I went, where there were others dressed even more oddly than me, so all started well. I dared hope, *would this be a fun day at school?*

Well, yes and no.

Turns out freshmen were mostly in grade nine, not eleven, so I looked a little out of place in classes that day. It wasn't bad. I think everyone thought I was cute. And Kevin was so involved in running the freshman week, he was too busy to make me do much of the idiocy he organized for everyone else. I just had to hang around and hold his books while he oversaw kids roll balls with their noses or carry eggs on spoons in races down the halls.

But at the end of the day he said, "I don't care that you did everything I said today, you'll be going to Kangaroo Court in the gym tomorrow, so dress the same and expect your punishment."

Now again, why would I do that? Seriously, I can't remember what I was thinking.

So the next morning I got up and dressed stupid again, and went back to the bus stop.

Today, a younger-looking student, not dressed up and probably in grade ten, ran over to me while we waited for the bus.

"Woo-hoo, a girlie slave! Here's a sample of what you can expect today," he hooted, and then, right to my face, he undid a bottle of perfume and still facing me, poured it all over my head. I just stood there, too shocked to be angry.

I didn't move. The syrupy liquid dripped all over my hair and down my T-shirt. The boy laughed and backed away, probably expecting some reaction, some lashing back. But I still didn't move, except for a little hand motion to wipe at my face. The smell was sickening, and the alcohol tang started to sting my eyes. The boy got a little uncomfortable. The other kids at the bus stop weren't laughing. I silently shook my head and wiped off my hands what I could of that stinking wet mess, then calmly turned my back on the boy and the bus stop and head held as high as possible, I walked back across the street to my house, where I slammed into the PMQ to my mother's questioning looks.

"I'm not going to school today. No way. I'm going to shower right now."

Now, the thing is, I loved school—always had, still wanted to. I can't remember missing a day of school for anything less than true illness. I hadn't complained about the slave auction, nor would I have. But that morning, showered and changed, I told my shocked mother what was going on at the school, and she quietly listened. I don't remember how we spent the day, but I felt no guilt about my first day of skipping out. I don't know what my mother did. You have to remember, this was an army base. Dependent wives, mothers and daughters didn't have much authority against a big military high school, where the disciplinarian vice-principal was a retired army colonel. No one dared to complain about such things because it might reflect on your father's career. We were well-trained dependants after all.

The next school day, Monday, all back to normal, I heard that the Kangaroo Court I'd missed had gotten quite out of hand, and due to complaints from certain parents, initiation week for freshmen was cancelled for the following year.

It never happened again, as far as I know.

If this had been the only instance when I suspected my mother speaking up for me or my brothers against the military school system, I might have disregarded the connection. But the following conversation on the phone took place one early spring day when I was in Grade 12. I had skipped out the afternoon from school to hitchhike into Pembroke, the nearest city, with my boyfriend, Don. He needed a new hockey stick for the weekend. I'd just come home. Mom answered the phone. I listened.

"Yes, hello Mr. Vice-Principal. Yes, I know Michele took the afternoon off school. It's Friday, she told me she arranged it with her teachers . . . that's right, there's no problem here. Goodbye."

I don't know how many times in a lifetime one has to say this, but again, Thanks Mom!

1975: Hockey Trip to Elmira

*A*t seventeen, Don, my hockey-playing boyfriend, earned one of the three civilian spots on the Base team, where he played with the military men for two years. He was not only the youngest player on the team, but also probably in the entire league. For me at sixteen, it was the start of my hockey-wife career, which would morph later into my hockey-mom life. Here's a fun little story of one of the trips.

"Wake up, Michele, get up!"

I don't remember who was shaking me, but I do remember waking up. The large dormitory room was hazy with smoke, and the heavy wooden door to the room where about six of us hockey "wives" were sleeping was wide open. People were milling around, half-dressed and chattering urgently, sounds echoing in the creaky high-ceilinged hallway.

I jumped up, already decent in shorts and a T-shirt, to find everyone getting dressed. It was about five in the morning, brightening outside through the thick, tall window glass. And obviously, the huge Victorian-style fraternity house that the Base Petawawa men's hockey team had been given to use as a hotel for that weekend's exhibition game against the Elmira New York's college team, was on fire.

The weekend had started normally enough on a big luxury bus with a toilet in the back. The team had a good budget because the manager was the Base Physical Education and Recreation Officer (BPERO), who had been incidentally, my father's boss, which was the main reason I'd been allowed to go along for the overnight trip. It had been quiet on the six hour drive down; the guys did have a game that Saturday evening. Most of them napped while the wives and girlfriends, like me, chatted. This was an extra weekend trip aside from the usual league games played around Ottawa for the Senior Men's league that the *Petawawa Stags* played in, a kind of "reward" trip to the States, to play an exhibition game against the Elmira College team. And to get to stay overnight was even better. In deference to the girlfriends along (that would be me, again), all women including the wives had agreed to share a dorm room with single beds. The guys were going to stay in their own dorm rooms away from us.

It was a big arena with a big crowd, bigger than what was a normal turnout for Men's Senior hockey back home. There was even an announcer, who mispronounced the French guys' names; very amusing! The game was exciting with the noisy college crowd, the play was quick. We won.

So that night was party time in the big frat house. Delivery pizza, beer, and card games. I went to bed early while the music, drinking, and smoking carried on downstairs.

But I guess someone fell asleep on his mattress with his cigarette still going. That's what I understood had happened as soon as I joined the crowd in the hall peering into the large community-style washroom. Some of the guys had a twin mattress standing on end in the claw-footed bathtub, while another was trying to hand-sweep shower head spray around to fully soak it. I think the water made it smoke up even more, thick and black. Coughing my way back to the room, I quickly dressed and packed and joined everyone else outside. A pink sunrise was just coming up as the blaring firetruck screech-stopped on the soggy spring lawn beside us.

I don't know if Elmira College ever invited a Canadian Base Hockey team back again.

*H*mmm . . . *just when I thought I was so grown up and mature, what with hanging out with "adults" and all.*

REFLECTION ON GROWING UP

*A*s I got older, I understood more about the differences between our base life and the rest of society, and I started to notice the effects those differences had had on us base kids. Moving around as much as we did, we became adaptable. Or rebellious. I knew one family that got kicked out of PMQs because their teenage son was caught stealing from locker rooms at the gym. They had to leave the base and move to the nearest civvie town—a huge disgrace and hardship for the family to give up the subsidized PMQ rent in those days of lower military pay.

Some of us were both adaptable and rebellious. My best friend Patti moved away from Yorkton before the end of the school year when I was in grade nine. She came back the following summer for a short visit as her family was passing through; we only had a couple of afternoon hours to hang out before they resumed their road trip.

"Let's go to Teen Town," she'd said. I assumed she wanted to see as many of her friends as possible on such a short visit. But, when we got there, she walked directly into the kitchen—remember, this was a community hall attached to the church—where the expensive turn-table record player and albums were kept. Only senior teenagers, that is, the Teen Town "executives," were permitted in the kitchen. Only they could touch the record player.

Patti walked right in, went right to the record player and turned it off. Casually browsing the albums, she'd asked, "What do you want to listen to?"

"Patti, what are you doing? Here comes Rick. We gotta go!"

"Who cares? What are they gonna do? I don't even live here anymore!"

Patti put on an album and cranked the volume, but some older boy was yelling at us through the pass-through counter to the kitchen, so I grabbed Patti's arm and yanked her out with me to run to the hall, back out to the heat and sunshine of the day. Patti had laughed as we ran. I was slightly concerned. I still lived there. Later in life, I would recognize Patti's actions, and what caused them. She was suffering from FIGMO, a state common in the military and in the military's followers: "Fuck It, I Got My Orders," meaning, who cares anymore about this place—I'm moving on. Kind of not a good life habit to acquire.

Another difference, maybe good, maybe not, was that generally, we did seem to grow up faster than I remember my civilian friends or cousins doing. I think back to those dances!

As a girl growing into a young woman I noticed other differences of base life. The military was (maybe still is) by nature a male-dominated, paternalistic culture. I know that most of Western society shared this issue, but it was now the 1970s and the Women's Liberation movement had made advances in many areas. We could plan on having incomes of our own instead of submitting to marriage to be the housewives our mothers were. Careers were starting to be an option; careers like Teacher, Stewardess, and Secretary were still common choices, but they were better than nothing! We could smoke and drink and get into the same places that men could. But military bases were behind the times in many regards, especially in gender equality. We had one big boss in charge—the base commander. You followed the rules of the base, by order of said commanding officer. And in the days I grew up, said COs were men. Women existed in the military and were making inroads into the military culture, but had a long way to go. Even those brave first women had a hard, tough reputation. The military was never offered as a career choice to me or my high school girlfriends that I recall.

My father was a physical training instructor and worked at the Base Rec Centre which always included at least a gym, pool, and arena. So even as a girl I always had had access to any sports activity or facility. My dad ran them; who would kick me out? My parents were fair, and my mother especially always encouraged her daughter as much as her boys to do anything she wanted. Who would stop me—I was also an eldest! But I do remember the sign on the weight room in Petawawa which I began using as an undersized fifteen year old trying to bulk up for lifeguard classes. It read: *Men Only. And Military Women.* As you can guess, I used it regardless, and it wasn't very long before the sign came down. But it was there once. And not that long ago, really. Within my own living memory.

As a lifeguard and swimming instructor, there was an incident where I was reminded of the ugliness of our base life, which I assume was a reality of the times everywhere then anyway.

"Where's Julia tonight?" I asked my class, "She missed

last week, too." I was seventeen, engaged to Don by now and in Grade thirteen, working four nights a week as a swimming instructor at Dundonald Hall Pool in CFB Petawawa. The class was usually comprised of young army wives, only a couple years older than me, most of them.

A woman looked sideways at her friend standing in the shallow end where we waded up to our waists. It was always a challenge getting these beginner women to get their hair wet.

"Well, I hear her husband is back from the field," she said. The Army guys were always away for days, even weeks, "in the field," training.

"So what?" I asked.

"You know, you're pretty young to be engaged," the woman said, looking at the little diamond ring I would still wear in the pool back then. "And maybe you don't understand how some things work. But some husbands don't like their wives going out in the evenings without them."

"Ha! You're kidding!" I said, "How could he stop her from taking a swimming class?"

But the women weren't joking and another one said, quite seriously, "Um, a couple of whacks with a broomstick and you wouldn't go out either."

So. Army husbands. There was no complaining allowed. My mother once told me that Army wives were tougher than Air Force wives. I had no idea what she meant then.

This incident helped explain to me why alcohol and divorce rates in the military were so high.

Alcohol. Again, like the rest of society, it was and still is, and forever will be, a problem for some. But back in the days when the military made Friday afternoon mess meetings mandatory, when soldiers were expected to party hard together, when booze on base was subsidized . . . well, I don't remember many Friday night suppers with Dad, that's for sure. Alcohol was definitely a devil for many military families.

Enough said. It wasn't a good part of the military, and I'm happy to report that over the next decades that I spent following my husband in his Air Force career, there was change happening, and the alcoholic traditions mostly died out, at least the sanctioned ones. Good riddance.

1975: Cognac in Jail

This next story includes the author's dog's thoughts on the escapade, which of course have to be attributed to the author's imagination. The rest is true, though.

How long will I be stuck in this cage? I'm the only one here. I'm hungry. How could this happen? It's been years since I was a stupid young pup and got picked up like this. I was just out searching and escaped from the house with the kids in the morning on their way to school.

Mama hasn't been around for a couple of days. Where is she? Papa has been gone for longer than that, but I couldn't find him anywhere after he left either. Instead of my usual night patrol, I needed to look for her during the day for a change. And yesterday morning I did make the break. Big Sis had left before the boys, so I knew I could get out with them if I timed the open door. And I did.

There was no sign of Mama anywhere. I tried the usual rounds, but there sure are a lot more people out and about in the daytimes than after dark. I couldn't find as much garbage to snack on either; I kept getting shooed away. And then the guys in the uniforms showed up. I hate them, but they did have some toast and peanut butter. Who could refuse just a bite? I didn't know they'd close the van door on me. At least they left the toast. Now here I am. How will I ever get out and find Mama? My kids are never around during the day, and they didn't find me yesterday. This could be awhile. Might as well take a nap.

Michele sailed into their PMQ townhouse on the south side after taking the bus home from the Base Petawawa high school on the north side. She was seventeen, and in charge of her three younger brothers this week while their mother was in Germany visiting their army father who was on his mid-tour break. Canada had a peacekeeping mission in Egypt in 1975. Her mother, excited for the week away to see her husband, had nevertheless been hesitant to leave them all alone, but Michele was fiercely against any kind of sitter or nanny being assigned. She'd been babysitting her brothers since she was ten and on this she and they stood solidly together. They weren't babies, they were at school all day anyway, and could look after themselves. Mom had to agree. She was even proud of her unruly brood.

"Hey," Michele called out, "anyone home?" She knew her sixteen-year-old brother Mark was hanging out with buddies and probably wouldn't be around for supper, but she did expect her other two younger siblings, John and Jeffrey, to be home soon, demanding to be fed.

As she walked into the kitchen, Michele paused when she noticed the dog dish was still full of the Gainsburger she had put in that morning.

"Cognac?" she called, waiting for the family dog to come running. Cognac was named for the liquor, because he was that nice caramelly brown. She hadn't noticed him tied up outside on her way in. He was probably upstairs on Mom and Dad's bed. He'd been quite sulky since Mom left on Friday, but she'd never known him not to eat his breakfast. And what would he be doing in the house all day, anyway? The last person out in the morning was supposed to hook him up to his chain outside. She hadn't noticed on her way in if Cognac had broken the chain again or not. He was a smallish mutt, only about as high as a terrier, but quite solid and strong. When they were smaller, the kids had tried in vain to train him to pull them on toboggans and wagons, like a sled dog, but Cognac had never obliged, preferring to run back and hop on with them.

Her youngest brother Jeffrey banged in the front door.

"I'm home! What's for supper?" he bellowed with a voice bigger than his ten years warranted. Stomping straight to the kitchen, he joined Michele looking down at the dog dish.

"Hey, Jeff," Michele said, "Have you seen Cognac? Cognac!" She called around the corner up the stairs, "Come here!"

"I'll check," Jeffrey took the stairs two at a time. He hadn't taken off his runners.

"Not up here!" came the response. The PMQ was one of the largest styles, but they weren't hard to check out quickly. Upstairs was just a hallway with five doors leading to bedrooms and a single bathroom. No Cognac.

Clomping back down, Jeffrey and Michele decided neither of them had heard him yelping to be let in in the middle of the night from his usual prowl. Come to think of it, they didn't remember him begging to go out either. And was it just this morning that Michele had filled his dish? Or maybe yesterday? She'd been pretty busy getting ready for school and doing chores; she honestly couldn't remember when last she'd seen Cognac! Maybe John or Mark knew what was up. They made some Kraft Dinner and boiled wieners while they waited for their brothers to come home.

But John phoned that he was going to a friend's for supper then to his ball game, and no, he thought Jeffrey was last out this morning—didn't he tie up Cognac? No, he hadn't heard him go out or come in last night. And Mark, well, he lived his own life, as any sixteen-year-old boy was apt to do. Michele and Jeffrey ate their dinner while Michele decided what to do.

"Hello? Military Police?" asked Michele, "I'd like to report a missing dog. Yes, I'll hold."

Jeffrey hopped around her, "Is he there? Is he?"

On military bases, there wasn't a specific dog catcher. The MPs scooped up any strays and held them themselves. Who knew what they did with them if they weren't claimed?

"Hello, yes, he's a little brown dog," said Michele. "Well, golden actually. His name is Cognac . . . he is?" Michele nodded her head up and down to Jeffrey. "What? A fine? How much is that? And for two days of food? He's been there for *two* days?"

Michele and Jeffrey looked guiltily at each other. Jeffrey was starting to tear up.

"Can I come get him? Yes, we can come tonight," said Michele, "Six o'clock at the MP shack. What's the building number? Yes, on our way." She hung up, grabbed her bag where the emergency money from her mother was stashed, and she and Jeffrey took off for the north side of the base.

Which was quite a hike, really. But they knew the

shortcuts, across lawns of the PMQs—no one put up fences in military housing in those days—through the woods cutting down to the Petawawa river, back up to the road across the bridge, and to the north side where all the military facilities were.

It was June, the sun was still high. Michele and Jeffrey were breathless running to the MP building, which they found by following the gridlines of the laid out streets with their building numbers large and black against the standard whitewash. They got to the right one, indistinguishable from all the other low, square military buildings. There were no police cars or anyone around. The front door was locked. And then they heard barking.

Running around the side of the building, there was a high window. There had been nothing to stand on, so Michele boosted Jeffrey up to look in. The window was cracked open and with their noise and voices they must have riled up Cognac. They now heard the familiar barking inside increase to the whining tempo they recognized as their Cognac in trouble!

Jeffrey was crying now too. "Cognac, Cognac! You bad little doggie! We're here! We'll get you out! Mickey! Mickey!"

Just as Michele had to drop him—Jeffrey was getting big—a little Volkswagen Beetle pulled up to the side of the building. *What a sight we must be*, Michele realized. *Sweaty and scruffy from the run here, a spindly little kid and his big sister.* Michele straightened herself to meet the young man approaching out of the car. Was this the MP? He was young and not in uniform, and now a young woman stepped out of the car also and waited beside it. His wife?

"We're here for our dog, please," Michele declared with

all the dignity she could. Jeffrey was trying to control himself beside her, but couldn't stop whimpering, in tune with the mournful yelps coming from inside the building.

"Um, where are your parents? I thought I was talking to your mom on the phone."

"My mother is in Germany visiting my father, who's on tour in Egypt. You said there was a fine, and for the two days of food, how much again exactly?" Michele asked precisely. "Please, let us get our dog. He's barking himself hoarse." She was pleased at how controlled she sounded.

"Yes, sure, come on." Flustered, the young man unlocked the door and led them inside.

Cognac couldn't restrain himself; once out of the cage he went nuts licking and crying and slobbering all over Michele and especially Jeffrey, who was also crying and laughing and hugging. Michele turned back to the MP who must have had "dogcatcher" as a secondary duty, meaning he was junior and new at this job. Michele tried to hand over the cash.

"No, no way," he said, hands up. "The fine is suspended."

Michele tried to insist, but by then the young wife had walked over. "Where do you live?" she asked.

"South side, Dundonald Drive," Michele replied, noticing then that she had forgotten the dog leash. He didn't look like he would now, but they didn't dare trust Cognac not to bolt once he was free; although loving and cuddly in the house, he was pretty badly behaved outdoors. She realized that they could expect a long hunched-over haul back home taking turns just holding his collar. She and all her brothers had had plenty of uncomfortable experience with that!

The wife said, "We'll drive you."

The car ride back was a little scrunched with Michele and Jeffrey and Cognac in the back seat of that Beetle. The young couple, probably only a few years older than Michele herself, questioned them all the way home, probably wondering if the kids were abandoned or something. But Michele straightened them out and had all the right answers; they were a normal military family living a rather ordinary base life, after all.

When they got home, they fed and hugged and petted their beloved little golden Cognac.

Who accepted this homage happily, and plotted his next escape.

I can only assume he plotted, because he did escape quite a few times!

It still doesn't seem strange to me that four kids, teenagers and one pre-teen, were allowed to be left on their own for a week or two while their mother visited their deployed father on another continent. Everyone's family lived like this on army bases like Petawawa. But it does remind me why, as the eldest, I was especially responsible for my age.

And why, at eighteen, I got married when I didn't even have to! I was ready to run my own life.

PART THREE. MARRIED WITH CHILDREN.

1976-1977: BRANTFORD, ONTARIO. STRANGE NEW WORLD.

1977, Brantford, Ontario. My new young husband is playing his last year of eligibility in Junior hockey for the Brantford Aragon Penguins—named for the restaurant sponsor—and working at a ShopRite catalogue store. I'm working full-time as a swim instructor at the Brant Aquatic Centre, now renamed these many years later as the Wayne Gretzky Sports Centre. How the hell did two teen-aged base brats end up here? And where are we going?

I met Don in Madame Labarre's Grade 11 advanced French class at General Panet High School in CFB Petawawa, in the fall of 1973. At fifteen years old, I was moved up to the Grade 11 advanced program, meaning, I was expected to go on to the thirteenth grade that Ontario had in those days. Coming from Saskatchewan was yet another culture shock in a lifetime of a military father's postings. It seemed to be getting harder the older I got—yes, I was starting to feel old at fifteen. In Yorkton, I had just finished Grade 9 in a civilian junior high school called Dr. Brass. Going to this huge base high school of grades nine to thirteen, where I was now a year younger than my classmates, was a real jump to young adulthood, that's for sure. But this move would not be the hardest I would experience—that would happen after leaving Petawawa, not arriving.

Don had suffered the French class as long as he could to meet "the new girl." As the only male student in dragonish Madame's class, the teacher was especially hard on him. It wasn't long before we were high-school sweethearts; he had a mustache. This impressed me greatly. We graduated Grade 12 together, and although his RSM father was posted that summer to Brantford to work with a reserve unit, Don remained in Petawawa and supported himself. But there was not much civilian work in Petawawa or even Pembroke for an inexperienced Grade 12 graduate, so he eventually joined his family in Brantford and got a job in a store. I stayed engaged throughout my grade thirteen year, which I also spent working as a lifeguard and swim instructor, and we were married in October 1976.

Then what?

I had always been an honour-roll student, and when elected Valedictorian by my classmates, I got called to the office to meet the principal. He was surprised that he didn't know who I was. I hadn't applied to any universities because my sole plan for the future was "to get married." The guidance counsellor had suggested that I not bother with the Calculus course I was struggling with, because it was pulling my average down, and what did I need it for anyway—I wasn't going to university, right? Such was the career advice to young women in the 1970s. But I had some inclination to keep options open, and thank goodness I fought through and miraculously passed Calculus, as the credit eventually did come in handy.

But I get ahead of myself. That was farther in the future and not in mind at this time.

A lovely late October wedding occurred, which my mother had organized and planned completely by herself; her bride-to-be daughter hadn't had a clue. Many of my classmates came back from their first semesters away at universities to attend. The appointed day passed magically. I do remember the weather held off and was mild enough without jackets, but that's about all I recall, being catered to and led everywhere that day. The morning after, however, was cloudy and threatened snow as Don and I headed away from Petawawa with my new in-laws to Brantford, to our first little apartment in the upstairs of an older home. My parents and brothers had sent me off, waving and crying from the front lawn of our PMQ. I can't remember feeling anything about leaving home— just numb. The drive to Brantford seven hours away was dreary and quiet, all the excitement and anticipation of getting married now over. I had no idea what kind of life awaited. I had never lived on "civvie street."

Bewildered but busy throughout November, I set up our little upstairs apartment nest with hand-me-downs, went shopping (mostly window shopping only), and wandered the new world of big city southern Ontario. It wasn't long before I applied for and started my job at the fantastic city pool, my credentials and experience eagerly accepted and welcome. I hadn't realized the excellent sports programs and certification opportunities I had taken for granted growing up weren't as cheap or available in this different world. On bases, our instructors had often been military trainers, and facilities had required little or no fees to use.

This unreal new life continued throughout that winter.

My job was great at the start—nine to three, Monday to Friday. I taught swimming lessons to school kids as part of their gym program, and did other classes for special-needs programs. My co-workers were mostly older women, which started me thinking, *Was this it? Slightly more than minimum wage and wearing a Speedo into menopause?* I liked working with the kids, but soon was looking forward to the weekends to get away from them. Then there were the swimmers who were elderly or had disabilities, such as being blind. This was all new to me. Anyone with special needs in those days didn't live on the bases where I grew up. I was discovering that I had lived a very sheltered, homogenous life until now.

I remembered a teacher from my Grade 13 English class who had come to General Panet to teach for his last year of his forty-year career, the previous thirty-nine having been spent at a public high school in downtown Montréal. He was as curious about our base life as we were about his stories of Montréal. We couldn't understand a world where some kids drove their own expensive cars to school in designer clothes while others lived on welfare with single mothers. The biggest difference in social class among students at my high school had been our father's rank: officer's kids were seen as the upper crust. But even they lived in PMQs, like the kids of corporals. And nobody had designer clothes or fancy cars. The only rich kids I knew in high school were the drug dealers, and they lived their own life apart from the rest of us, mingling with the townies. There were no single mothers living on the base that I recall. I knew families split up in those days, as they always have, but when they did in my world, their mothers took the kids away with them, to live in the civilian world.

They weren't missed; turnover in our classes every year was at least 30 percent, and it was not unusual for kids to come and go throughout the school year.

So, living in Brantford was like being "Alice-in-Wonderland" for me. Rich people. Poor people. Older people and other kinds of people. It was a shock and a wonder.

We didn't have a TV in those cozy first months, so for entertainment I would watch my husband's evening hockey practices. Weekends there were games and as the only wife on the team, I was privileged to be allowed on the team bus, which wasn't as wonderful as you might think—a school bus-load of high-spirited boys aged sixteen to nineteen whooping it up and sneaking beers for the ride home. I had grown up with enough boys and didn't find them at all amusing. But I did enjoy a ready-made social life with the hockey team. I sat with the other girlfriends and sisters at games. There were parties at player's houses, most if not all of whom lived with their parents in what I considered mansions. We had a Christmas party at the magnificent home of one the Italian kids on the team. It had a marble foyer with a staircase curving up to sumptuous heights, chandeliers glowing. We ate snacks and sipped sparkly drinks in a reception parlour of sorts with a showy fireplace. People in black and white served us. I had never been to an event like this, especially in someone's home. The people were different somehow. The girls were prettier, their fancy dresses more elegant, the boys clean-cut and handsome in suits with shiny ties, their mothers richly coifed and bejewelled and manicured. It was incredible, like being in a movie. I floated in this atmosphere of strangeness, this different orb of tinkling glass and soft, golden light.

And Don and I figured out soon enough this kind of life was not for us, not long term, certainly not yet. Don was laid off from his store job in the spring and applied for various positions, but eventually we returned full circle, and in June of 1977, he was off to Cornwallis, Nova Scotia to do his basic training in the military. As former army brats, we knew enough that he should join the Air Force and not the Army of course, even though these were the amalgamated years of the Canadian Armed Forces and Don might have been tricked easily enough to get a "green" (army) trade. We both knew what the Army life meant—extra moves and away time in the field. Even our army fathers encouraged the Air Force over the Army, and especially over the Navy! I went with Don to the recruiter, who tried to cajole me to join up also—this was quite a surprise but quotas for women in the military must have been starting, I assume now, and with my grade thirteen certificate, I could have been an officer. But I had other plans by then. My boss at the pool in Brantford ran the Aquatic Centre from a wonderful desk in her own office with a door she could close, and where she wore nice clothes to work, like panty-hose and heels. I found out she had a university degree in Recreation, so that sounded great to me. I would go to university. Like I had once promised my mother I would someday do, on the day I came home from school in grade thirteen wearing my diamond ring. I would get a degree so I wouldn't have to keep wearing a bathing suit to work.

I joined Don in Winnipeg after his basic training. He had a trades training course to do there, a course he would graduate from at the top of his class. This would give him a choice in our first posting. I stayed with an aunt that fall. I worked at various city pools, wherever I could get shifts, like Sargent Park, Sherbrooke, and the overwhelming Pan Am, which was even bigger than the Brant Aquatic Centre.

I also signed up at the University of Winnipeg and took some classes, having been accepted with a required science credit, which was that good-old Calculus course. We were on our way.

1978: Edmonton, Alberta. The Locker Room.

*D*on finished his Winnipeg trades training in December of 1977. After driving in our little Chevy Vega to visit my parents in their new posting of Chilliwack, British Columbia for Christmas, we headed to our new home in Edmonton, Alberta. The tiny two-bedroom shoe-box PMQ we pulled up to in Lancaster Park, CFB Edmonton, looked like a castle compared with the months of living in a spare room at my aunt's. Glistening silver (aluminum) siding reflected sunlight on the snowy prairie field across the street. Our first home. Again, of course. My life had many firsts, you see!

The following scene reminds me of how I hadn't just grown up, I had grown. There'd be more of that. In fact, does it ever end?

The young women weren't threatening me, not exactly, not yet. I'm just back to the steamy locker room, around the corner from the showers, towelled up, at the end of the late shift with my co-lifeguard, Claude, who had already closed up and gone on his way to the Men's. My dripping Speedo is where I left it to go shower, lying on the varnished wood bench just behind the women standing in front of me now.

Not really women, girls themselves, I see, about my own age—20, 21—all in the short buzzy haircuts and tattoos which were not yet common on women in the late 1970s. Not common that is, except on military bases, and on young military females. *This is CFB Edmonton, north of the city proper, and only an air base, so no real problem,* I reason with the arrogance of a former army brat. I'd seen tougher.

The wider girl, tacky rose tattoo showing on her right boob above her bra, says to me, "Is this your fucking bathing suit making the floor all wet?"

Oh, I get it. They do think they're tough. Especially three of them together. I probably look like a skinny little girl in my towel and stringy wet hair, but I've had my own lifeguard training, and I also use the weight room, which in those days, was not that welcoming to women. I'm filling out, I'm in good shape. I'm 20.

"Well, yes, I have to admit there is quite a puddle," I tell them. "But this is a locker room, you know." I say this sweetly. "I promise to wipe it up with paper towel later."

Rose Tattoo doesn't move, so I turn my back to her and open my locker—nobody locked up back then—and now, mostly drip-dried, I deliberately drop the towel and reach for my own underwear.

Another one asks, "What unit are you with?"

"I'm not in the military," I say, back still turned to them. "My husband is a Met Tech in Air Operations."

"Oh, how nice for you, a kept woman and all. Don't you do anything?" Rose Tattoo taunts.

"I go to university."

"La-de-da. You must think you're pretty smart. Lucky your husband pays for you."

By now I'm mostly dressed except for socks—the floor is wet after all—so I saunter over to the washroom area and get a handful of paper towels, all the while chatting them up as if we were all new friends. Big Rose moves a little, to let me by.

"You're right," I say, "I am lucky. But it's hard, too, going to university and working nights and weekends while my husband does shift work and tries to work on his own degree part-time. He wants to be an officer. He plays on the base hockey team. I lifeguard and work full-time in the summer. I play sports. We have no family in Edmonton. Do you?"

The follower girls are backing off, getting dressed, mumbling, not so sassy anymore. One mentions that she works at Base Ops, too. Another says tryouts for women's soccer are coming up. Rose Tattoo hesitates, then starts dressing herself. They're just locker-room girls, after all, like me, lonely and far from hometowns, getting by, making lives. None of us is really so tough. We're all pretty tough.

Leaving the Rec centre, I glance behind me. I don't think they will follow me out, but once I step away from the leaking light of the building, the high prairie night sky a clear velvet black stabbed with starlit points of light, I take a deep breath, and run all the way home.

I do make the soccer team that spring.

*T*he three and a half years in Edmonton were a whirlwind of work, school, Wednesday night discos at the junior ranks *mess, hockey games, house parties. Buying a better car. Getting into the University of Alberta. Getting my National Lifeguarding qualifications so I could work for the city of Edmonton pools, and at union wages, no less!*

Living, laughing, loving. Improving and moving forward. And still so young!

LEMON TO LEMONADE

*B*y November 1978, I'd had a busy year in Edmonton. I worked as a lifeguard. Was the Summer Recreation Supervisor for the kids' program. Started a four-year Bachelor's program at the University of Alberta in Recreation Administration.

Our 1973 Chevy Vega was rusting away and we wanted to go to Ottawa for Christmas for Don's parent's twenty-fifth wedding anniversary. No way would the Vega make that trip back east from whence it had originated, in Brantford, back a lifetime ago it seemed, in early 1977. It had been listed in that gravelly used car lot at $1800, but I, at eighteen years-old, had "negotiated" it down to $1750. I'm still proud. But its lifetime was up, so now with money saved for the down payment and high hopes for a good trade-in value, Don and I headed out one bitterly cold evening after work and school, into the city to shop for a new car.

"I see it has 'cancer.' This is an eastern car, isn't it?" the salesman told, more than asked, us.

I was offended. "Maybe some rust, sure," I agreed, "But it runs okay. It must be worth something in trade?"

We'd just test-driven a blue Buick Skylark, not brand new, but close enough. It hadn't started well in the cold, and it had chugged along for the first part of the drive, so I wasn't eager. It was a pretty car, though. A shiny pearly blue that glowed under the high fluorescent lights in the lot. It was dark already at 6:00 p.m. in Edmonton, in November.

"I'm afraid it's not worth anything. We'll take it off your hands and not charge to send it to the junk yard. But hey, what about the Skylark? A beauty, right? You're in the military, Don. You should have no problem with the loan."

I was leery. Did he have anything else to show us? I didn't like the sound of the Skylark, no matter that the salesman assured us it just needed to be warmed up before driving.

"Not on my lot here," he said, "But go up the road to the Oldsmobile dealer. I know them; I'll call ahead. They might have something for you there."

So we left, and, no surprise, the other place had a beautiful 1977 Olds Omega, white and clean with a blue landau roof, pulled up in front, and already running. Purring. Ready for us to test-drive. Whereupon it of course performed wonderfully—why not? The dealers had been in contact (I think the correct term is "in cahoots"), and Oldsmobile Guy was smooth and ready for us. Of course we fell for it hook, line, and sinker.

Off to Ottawa we went a few weeks later for our Christmas trip. What a drive—snow, cold, dark—much longer than I remember travelling from Brantford to Winnipeg two summers earlier. No radio stations for many of the miles, but we had our eight-track player. Bachman Turner Overdrive blaring away! And such a nice visit with the in-laws, who stuffed us with baked goodies and rich gravied-meals and handed us cash for our Christmas present. In the days before we had credit cards, cash could not be under-appreciated. Turns out we'd need every penny for the drive home, though.

I can't list all the mechanical failures we encountered on the trip back to Edmonton in that pearly white car. I didn't understand them all then, much less remember what they all were now. I wish I could make the trip sound funnier than it was, but even over thirty years later, I can't smile much about it. Suffice to say, it was a trip from hell in a pretty car from hell. We needed a screwdriver to open something (maybe the carburetor) under the hood every time, just to start the creature. The weather turned arctically cold. The heater stopped working. I had to scrape the inside windshield while Don drove. On New Year's Day we stopped at an RCMP detachment to ask where we could get gas; in those days everything was closed for the holiday. We got ripped off on a replacement car battery in North Bay. Years later, some credit card company used a nightmare car trip as a commercial advocating their credit card for emergencies. I wondered how they knew our exact story! Then we had to replace the crappy battery again in Kenora. By Winnipeg we were almost broke, and Don had to get a personal cheque cashed in the Junior Ranks Mess there—banks were closed and there were no such thing as instant tellers. They had a twenty-five dollar maximum allowed on personal cheques. We used every cent of it for gas back to Edmonton. I bought a loaf of bread to eat for the last day of the trip home.

We made it, though, young and strong as we were. Safe and sound. And furious about the lemon we'd bought. Back we went to the dealer to complain, but in 1978, it was "buyer beware," especially for sucker kids such as ourselves. They did offer to diagnose and fix it for us, but of course we couldn't afford, or trust, the dealer. We would find a friend of a friend to fix it as best he could in his home garage.

But we learned our lesson. We never bought a used car again. And now we were super motivated to save and work hard to pay off this junky car, and buy a new one.

Our horrid experience would lead us to our dream car in the spring of 1980, when we would convince the bank manager that we could handle the bigger loan for the Datsun 200SX.

And when the Datsun salesman asked us if we wanted to check the Olds one last time for any personal possessions, I practically ran away from him, afraid he'd back out of the deal, exclaiming as I jumped into the beautiful new black sporty car we'd just bought, "No way. It's your problem now! Bye!"

*A*nd that wonderful new car lasted us seven years. We loved it. Oh, and we got a credit card as soon as we could, too.

And I still cannot smile much about this story.

You'd think we would have learned more of a lesson from it, but not exactly. Young military folk are such easy prey. We would get suckered on our first couple of house buys years later, too!

1981: KINGSTON, ONTARIO. FROM THERE TO HERE.

*W*hen my corporal husband Don was selected to go to Royal Military College (RMC) for his degree, it was too good an opportunity to pass up, even though it meant I would leave the University of Alberta with only three years of my four-year degree completed. I'd considered staying in Edmonton by myself to finish, but in the end decided that the Recreation Degree might not have as profitable a future as originally envisioned, and so, like most university students, I changed my mind about my major. I would follow Don to Kingston and seek my new fortune there.

Spoiler alert: It did work out for the best—it usually does! I'm not an "everything happens for a reason" person, but I am a "make lemonade out of lemons" one. A lesson I was still learning in this story.

I'm not too old yet, and lucky to still not look my age, although I didn't appreciate it enough back then. I appear younger than 23. Even with three years of university behind me, two years before that of working full-time on and off as a swim instructor/lifeguard, and throughout the already many military moves with my high school boyfriend/husband, I'm not out of place in this college classroom, in a program called Business Administration, Data Processing. Years later, I would have to explain that meant Computer Programming, not data entry, but those future years were not imagined yet.

Someone who introduced herself as Maya or Moira is sitting beside me in the two-seater desk, as intent as the rest of us thirty or so students, listening to and watching a short female teacher, in a blazer and pants—how professional she looked—write some sort of list on the blackboard.

"And in your third year, these are the core courses," she said, scratching with the old-style white chalk on the blackboard. (It *was* black. How modern! They all used to be green.)

"Maya (or Moira)," I whispered and poked to my seatmate's obvious annoyance, "What does she mean by 'third year'?"

"What do *you* mean? She's talking about the course requirements in third year!"

"But I'm not supposed to be in any three-year program. Just the two-year one!"

This is Kingston, Ontario, 1981. My corporal husband, excuse me, Officer Cadet Husband, is about to start at Royal Military College, which was a great opportunity for him to earn his degree and become an officer. We had just arrived from Edmonton barely a week earlier, three years of my four-year Recreation Administration degree at the University of Alberta now left unfinished. Despite my excellent grade point average there, Queen's University in Kingston had no comparable program, and I had figured out there wasn't much future in that field for a military wife leaving communities every three or so years anyway.

Now, what is a systems analyst? I'd seen them advertised in the want ads for over thirty thousand per annum. If I could ever make $30,000 a year, wow, that would be the goal! So, down the street to St. Lawrence College I went, where those excellent grades from Alberta had assured me a last-minute registration in whatever program could lead to such a lucrative job title, whatever it means!

And now here I sit.

Maya (or Moira) answers, "There's no two-year program. It's three years long. Unless you mean the twelve month Junior Programmer course?"

No, that's not what I mean. I'll need to work over the summers. And this is not Alberta, with their two-year college diplomas, as I've now discovered. It's Ontario, who because of the old grade thirteen system, has to run the programs for three years for the Grade twelve graduates. *Great.* I'll be stuck at school for another three years before graduating with any hope for a good job at $30,000 per year. After six years of post-secondary schooling, all on my own dime, I might as well have tried to become a doctor or lawyer! *This had better be worth it.* I sighed.

*O*ver thirty years later, I can finally smile at the memory of that clueless first day in that college classroom. Now retired from a long, successful career in Information Technology, I must admit, yes, it was worth it. I finally made thirty thousand dollars a year. Even more.

Goooal! (World Cup comes to mind . . .)

1981-1984: KINGSTON

*T*he years at college and Kingston were cultures way different from life at university and Edmonton. They were exciting years, filled with RMC events to attend with my husband Don, who was busy with his own degree program while playing Varsity hockey. I had a heavy course load for Computer Studies at St. Lawrence College, making lifelong friends during the process. Unlike university, I followed the same course schedule with my classmates for our three-year program, so naturally we all hung out together on the same timetable. Parties there were aplenty. A typical weekend would be a college pub night on Thursday, a home hockey game on Friday night, followed by hitting the bars in downtown Kingston; then Saturday night was likely to host a formal RMC event, for which I was required to wear a long gown. Whew, youth really is for the young! Sunday through Thursday was homework, study, workouts, classes. Long days and good sleeping nights. These were the years I did not watch TV. Hill St. Blues? Dynasty? I never saw an episode.

My memories of these times are full, multi-faceted and overlapping, like a collage. Here are some moments I've picked out.

*H*ow am I going to come to school in the winter with no plug-in for my car in the parking lot? I wondered desperately.

As usual, I had moved from one kind of place, Edmonton, to one with a completely different climate—Kingston. It was muggy and humid here on Lake Ontario, the last days of August before the September long weekend, and I was running the last hoops of bureaucratic requirements to attend St. Lawrence College. Errands, book buying, class schedules, even teacher interviews to get exemptions for elective courses: back in 1981, before our online world of today, these things all needed personal attention and hand-delivery. I was almost done at the administration counter paying my tuition and asking about parking. Don and I had bought a brand new snazzy black Datsun 200SX coupe the year before—my dream car. It had a cassette player with auto-reverse. I would be driving that car to school every day, as I had needed to drive to the University of Alberta in Edmonton. City buses never did routes into the bases where we lived in PMQs. And now I had just been told that, no, there were no parking fees here at St. Lawrence. There was a large, free parking lot for students. I should have no problem getting a spot every day.

"No, sorry, but I'll need a paid spot with a plug-in," I said, trying to clarify.

"No, dear," the clerk repeated, "we don't have plug-ins for any of the parking."

I couldn't believe it! No plug-ins? I was rather worried. What about the cold winter days when my car wouldn't start after sitting in the parking lot all day while I was in class? I needed to pick up my husband after school.

This sounded like a deal-breaker. Who ever heard of free student parking and no plug-ins? Ridiculous!

But the kind, amused lady behind the counter smiled and assured me that I would not be needing any plug-in or boost for my car during the winter. Honest.

And of course, she was right. It would never get to the winter temperatures in Kingston that Edmonton took for granted. I should have learned to be more trusting, but then, the first day of snow happened.

"Who are you? Nanook of the North?"

What? I was dressed in my normal winter attire: full-length down-filled coat complete with duct-tape patching, tall skidoo-style boots, mitts, scarf, hat plus hood. Our neighbour took one look at me heading to my car that morning while she stepped outside in normal shoes, leather jacket, no gloves, and added, laughing, "It'll melt by noon."

And she was right, too.

College was not like university either. It was easier and it was harder. It was more fun. It was more work, more tests, more assignments. It was less personalized in terms of class selection; the diploma requirements were inflexibly laid out for everyone in the same program. It was more personal in terms of student attention. Class sizes were smaller, and became smaller every semester, as students flunked or dropped out.

Because the first year of my program had more electives to fulfill, and because I'd had three previous years of university whose credits could be applied towards those electives, I found myself with a light load that first year. Instead of the five or six courses per semester that I would be doing in second and third year, I only had three. But

I still had to pay full tuition to be in the program. Now, most students would love taking only three courses per semester, but I was not like most of my class; I had worked multiple jobs in summers in Edmonton to save money for school. Don was also working hard and his military pay sustained our lives: housing, car loan, food, bills. We were getting by, but no way was I going to "waste" my full tuition on just a part-time course load.

"Can I take another course, for interest?" I asked the advisor.

"Of course, if there is room. What are you thinking about?"

"Well, I never got enough science credits in high school. How about a chemistry or physics class?"

"Sure. The technologist program has a first year physics course that'll fit with your schedule. Enjoy yourself!"

And it was kind of a cool course. It wasn't, however, what I'd expected. There was not a lot of theory, just many paragraphs-long descriptions of real-world problems, like, angles of wheelbarrow ramps and weights and capacities, how long to fill, how much to carry, and stuff like that. The formulas were provided. And we worked on the solutions together in class, teamwork-style. The tests were easy to calculate. One time, we were marking a test together in class, and as usual, I was getting all correct answers. They were multiple choice, for heaven's sake—simple.

But I guess not everyone thought so, and on this day, during discussion of the test, a sulky boy sitting behind me, complained out loud, "What are you doing in this class anyway? You're not in our program!"

"I'm taking it for fun. I'm in Computer Programming."

"Who takes a course like this for fun?"

I started to feel a little uncomfortable. This guy—and 90 percent of the students in this program were guys—was jealous and resentful of my smarts in "his" program. I was the outsider here, a familiar position that I had been forgetting in my academic life.

I decided not to continue the discussion. I completed the course and relearned a lesson: Some people are unaccepting of outsiders. Move on.

Back to my own program. In second semester I decided to take some courses at Queen's while my St. Lawrence course load was still light enough. Maybe someday I would go back to university for a degree in Computer Programming, after my diploma from college. Such was my bias still, thinking university was "better" than college. I'd been learning to keep my options open; who knew where and when I'd end up and what I'd need there? A valuable lesson from living in the military.

But the programming course I took at Queen's was taught by a nerdy, uncommunicative grad student, who couldn't teach a rock to roll down a hill. The class was in an auditorium that held hundreds, and the grade was based on only two tests: midterm and final. I'd already had a full semester of being better taught at St. Lawrence, so by applying that learning to this university course, I, unlike more than half the class, passed.

I never did follow up with the university degree; I would never need to. My college diploma would turn out to be the best decision of my working life. In fact, the first full-time job I got after graduation, working a summer for a geologist who was creating his own software out of his basement office, I got by answering an ad in the Kingston paper.

The geologist, after hiring me, and paying me more as a part-time recent graduate than I'd ever made as a lifeguard, said, "I could have hired a Queen's grad for this job, and some who applied even said they'd work for free for the experience, but I was told that if you want a solid programmer who can follow specs, hire a St. Lawrence grad."

It was the start of a great career.

There were many great times at St. Lawrence. I met my lifelong best friend, Judy, in second year. Here's a quote:

"Who wants to skip class with me and go to the Pub?"

Self-explanatory, right?

The following quote, however, was a reminder that I was still a military wife despite enjoying the college-student life:

"Please hand over the batteries from your Walkmans, ladies."

There was another base brat in my class named Mandy. Her parents were posted in Germany while she'd stayed back in Kingston for school. She was a quiet girl, studious and classically attractive with blond wavy curls, always well-dressed, unlike me in my t-shirts and runners wardrobe. I was a bit in awe of her and her poise. Although she didn't party and pubcrawl in my circle, we of course were classmates, and she knew I was married and lived on base. So for March break in third year, we decided to go to Germany together on the free military flights that dependants could use if there was room, and if you had the necessary earned "points." My husband had earned enough for one of us to take the trip, so while Mandy was going on her father's points to visit her parents, I would visit my brother, Mark, who was posted at this time in Baden, Germany, with his new young wife, Lorain.

Now this was 1984. Sony Walkmans were all the rage. Clunky and funky as they would seem today, they were the slickest music technology of the time. Mandy had one. I borrowed one. We had our cassettes in our purses, and we settled into seats on the Boeing 707 in CFB Trenton, ready to relax and plug into headphones for the flight's duration.

"Please put those away for takeoff," the Air Force stewardess warned. We did.

"No electronics on military flights," said the next corporal, once we were up and enroute.

"But why? They're just Walkmans."

And that's when we were reminded that this was not a commercial flight. They took our batteries. No argument, no questioning of authority. *Just like old times*, I sighed to myself with a flash of insight. There was more to "real" life than living in a paternalistic "nanny" state of military regulation. The rest of the flight was long and boring, as I recall.

Free flights sound great, but other than that one to Germany, Don never did earn enough points for a dependable trip for the two of us. I had tried once from Edmonton to go to British Columbia because my parents by then were posted in Chilliwack, and although I made it there, I was "bumped"—displaced by a higher-priority passenger—coming home. The cost of the last-minute flight back was more than if I'd taken a planned return trip! So while in Kingston, I only got to visit my parents at Christmas, which we paid for with Canada Savings Bonds frugally deducted directly from Don's pay throughout the year and redeemed in the fall.

I had adapted to Kingston and my college life there. But subtle changes were underway. My best friends now were all "townies," that is, Kingston home-towners. While other students went back to where they came from for the summer, and while Don was doing military summer training away in places like Borden, Ontario, I stayed and worked and hung out with Judy, Dan and Rory, and Lisbeth from Kingston. By graduation, we'd become a family and stayed in touch for years, until our own families of children came along. Kingston had become a new experience for me. I was starting to be able to imagine myself as someone from somewhere. I even thought about settling and retiring in Kingston, some far off future day.

Of course, it was not to be, not yet. And not Kingston.

1984: JOB INTERVIEW

Military wives have a tough time keeping a professional career going. First, the military member's "Profession at Arms" is priority number one—postings were for the military member's benefit only. In addition to the uprooting moves, there was also the subtle, and not even that subtle, prejudice against hiring a military spouse. As we see in this story.

"I see on your resume that you live on Queenston Heights? Where is that exactly?"

And with her answer—"On the base. Near Fort Henry,"—Michele sealed her fate: interview failed.

"Oh? Is your father military?"

"Well, yes, but I live here in Kingston with my husband. He's military too."

"Oh, okay then, thank you for coming in, Michele. Goodbye."

Confused, Michele stayed seated for another moment, wondering if she'd missed something. They hadn't asked her anything about the job yet. The four interviewers, seated at the far end of the boardroom table, smiled, nodded, and motioned for her to leave. And so Michele stood up, straightened the skirt on the overpriced suit-dress she'd bought for the occasion, thanked the nameless, faceless people in the room, and left.

Michele had graduated that spring from the Computer Science program at St. Lawrence College in Kingston, Ontario, With Distinction. She and her best friend Judy had calculated the exact number of courses over the three-year program in which they'd need to get A's to qualify for that lofty addendum to their diplomas, and they'd made it. They'd even overdone it and each received one extra A for good measure. Their working motto in those fun college years had been "Most amount of money for least amount of work". They fully expected to get good paying jobs someday, but wanted to enjoy the college experience along the way.

And now, Michele was ready. Her resume had been promoted by her teachers and selected with a few others for a coveted interview with the Ontario Health Insurance Program—the old OHIP—who had recently moved a major data centre to Kingston and was looking to hire entry-level programmers. A dream job for anyone from her class. Michele was extra excited for the opportunity. Her husband had just technically failed out of RMC. "Technically," because he'd reached a limit on exam rewrites in his third year. This meant he could return to repeat his third year, but at his own expense. An expense which, if Michele could get this job at OHIP, they would be able to afford.

So, Michele was ready. She had the grades. She'd been voted "best interviewee" in their job preparation classes. She even had relevant summer job experience from the Dupont factory in town. She was polite, personable, and prepared for the interview.

But what she wasn't prepared for was the automatic

dismissal as a candidate because of her husband's military career.

So Michele learned her lesson. Forced to quit RMC, her husband Don was returned to the rank of corporal in his old trade of Meteorology and posted to Winnipeg, where he would eventually earn his degree on his own time at the University of Manitoba. And where Michele would land another prestigious job interview at one of the "100 Best Places to Work" of the time: the Great-West Life Assurance Company.

She would start the interview there herself, professionally dressed in that same smart suit-dress, with the words, "You will notice my diploma is from Kingston, Ontario. If you're wondering why I ended up here in Winnipeg, it's because my husband is in the military. And even though we do move around in the military, I can guarantee you at least three years of dedicated time at work here, which I challenge any other applicant to promise."

Michele did get the job at GWL; her bosses later told her they had been very impressed with her interview.

A *nd we did stay in Winnipeg for almost seven years, the longest time I had ever lived in one place in my whole life up until then. I loved my job, advancing in levels from Junior Programmer to Intermediate Analyst and up to a Senior Systems Analyst at Great-West Life, finally finding out what a real systems analyst did. I also noticed that others who had been hired with me had come and gone during those years. Don did get his degree and became an officer again, in his own new career of Logistics. Thank goodness for the prejudice*

at OHIP—it taught me how to handle that particular career hurdle. There'd be more hurdles, though. Life's like that!

1984-1991: WINNIPEG, MANITOBA. REAL LIFE AND GAMES.

*A*rrival in Winnipeg was a low point for a couple of reasons. For one thing, Winnipeg, Manitoba in October is not a picturesque place, nothing at all like the colourful fall splendour that we'd driven away from in waterfront historic Kingston a week earlier. Grey, windy, cold, it was a working-class big town in the middle of the country. It was also a low point in my husband's career. He was back to the rank of Corporal again after doing three years in RMC as an officer cadet where we'd had a three-bedroom officer's PMQ. In Winnipeg, I cried when we saw the grubby stucco story-and-a-half where the bathroom only had an old tub without a shower. My hand pushed through soggy drywall the first time I leaned against that wall to put the plug in.

But as with every move, this was the one step back before the two steps forward. All was not gloom, despite the naked windy streets of our new city. I had my diploma. Don had his Logistics Officer Training completed. And it was still just the two of us, no babies yet.

We're not even thirty; life is just starting!

This next story is true but for a little creative license where my actual memory fails—did Freddie phone or show up at the door that day? No matter. The ball game was all real.

Sunday morning. Leicester Square, CFB Winnipeg, May 1985.

My husband and I usually slept late on Sundays, if not through to the afternoon, in those days. Young, no kids, no mortgage, living in military housing right on base. My husband, a corporal, was working on his degree part-time and I had my first grown-up job after college at the biggest private employer in town, becoming the IT professional I would retire as over 30 years later. Pretty good start-up life, it's easy to see now!

A beautiful sunny spring morning in Winnipeg. How many lovely mornings like that had we missed due to hang-overs from excellent drinking, partying Saturday nights? But not this Sunday. The black clunky phone was blaring downstairs. No voice messaging in those days. It wasn't giving up so I stumbled out of bed to answer it. It was remarkably bright downstairs in the tiny combination living dining room. *What time is it anyway?*

"Hey, Mickey, about time, it's almost nine. Get Don for me!"

"Who is this?" No call display, of course.

"Mickey, for fuck's sake, wake up Don. It's Fred. I need Don to meet me at the ball diamond on Ness at the end of the runway. Tell him to bring all his gear. As many gloves as he's got. I'm bringing some guys. Be there, like, now! I'm leaving right away."

And then he hung up.

Don groaned out of bed when I told him what Fred was up to. But Don was a great ball player and we were young, so he grabbed his shorts and followed me back downstairs and then down to the unfinished basement to get the ball gear bag.

"I didn't know Fred played ball. Does he have a glove?" he bellowed while putting the extra bats in the bag.

Good question. My cousin Freddie was a year older than me. Growing up I had considered him a cool guy who'd been knowledgeable about music and smoking and other exotic life experiences that I was not at all familiar with. But sports? I didn't really know, having grown up myself on military bases with all types of sports the main focus of life. I met Don, himself an army brat, in high school when he was a hockey star and ball player, before he joined up. Posted to Winnipeg now where Freddie lived, we rarely saw my cousin except at family events in nearby small prairie towns. Our lives didn't usually intersect socially at all.

"I don't know, he said bring everything."

And off we went.

The Game

Freddie and a bunch of guys on motorcycles and in muscled-up cars were already at the ball diamond when we showed up. There's a Tim Horton's there now, but I still remember it as I saw it that morning in 1985: the clear sky that brilliant wide blue, quiet on a Sunday morning at the end of the runway, surrounding fields that hadn't greened up from the gentle golden brown left after the winter melt. The diamond was in great shape, no bags or lines chalked yet, but level and softly gravelled, the huge metal chicken-wire backstop guarding Ness Road.

Freddie was running around, ordering, "Stand here, there, get off your bike, don't park there, put down your smoke!" Then he saw us pull up beside the field, and sprinted over.

"Hey man, good to see you. Hey, Mickey. Okay, I've dragged these assholes out for a baseball game, because, can you believe it, they say they've never played! I told them we'd teach them and I knew you lived near here, so help me before I kill some of them!"

Freddie is dressed in T-shirt and runners, but his buddies look like something from a '50s gang movie: tight jeans, black leather boots and motorcycle vests, chains hanging around belts. Lots of cigarettes going and bleary eyes blinking around, like they were on a foreign planet.

I can't recall much of a game happening. The morning passed with Freddie and Don playing everywhere, directing like traffic cops, showing guys how to hold the bat, where to stand, even which direction to run and that they should hurry! One guy did a perfect slide into second, not because he knew how, but because he slipped on his boot soles. Safe!

The morning fizzled out. Some heavily-eyelinered girlfriends showed up to take their guys home for breakfast or to go back to bed. Don and I collected gear, and said goodbye to Freddie.

It was a beautiful day, but we went home to sleep away the afternoon.

Fascinating how cousins in the same time and place lived in such different worlds. Yet still much in common, despite the diverse upbringings. I can't believe how many warm spring days we wasted back then, but it was so sunny in Winnipeg most of the time that like all young people, we thought we'd have forever to enjoy them. Some life lessons cannot be learned until you pass through them.

NOVEMBER 1985: NEW LIFE

"Oh my God!" Patti berated me, "You knew you were pregnant! That's why you weren't drinking last week when Judy was in town!"

Patti. Yes, the same Patti I knew in Yorkton. She and her sisters had settled in Winnipeg after their father had retired from the military and had moved them all back to Killarney, Manitoba. The same Killarney where my grandmother lived, and so we'd kept in touch from time to time over the years. And now we had renewed the best friendship of our youth. We were both young women with good jobs, setting up with normal life acquisitions, like store-bought furniture instead of hand-me-downs and paid-off cars. In fact, one of Patti's sayings was "We're just as poor as we ever were, but with better stuff." It was interesting meeting up with a childhood friend, skipping over the tough high school and university and college beginnings, to find each other again; everyone was progressing in their lives.

We partied on the weekends, went to dances at the mess, enjoyed downtown restaurants and bars. We played softball with the league at work in the summers and curled in the winters. I learned that Winnipeg, the hard-working-class city, was "a great place to live, but you wouldn't want to visit." Haha.

Life was pretty fun. And still no kids.

Yet. Well, that just changed. Yup, it's true I was ready for a family, but honestly, Patti, I didn't know I was pregnant that cold fall of 1985 when Judy—yes, the same best friend Judy from St. Lawrence College in Kingston, who now had her own job and boyfriend in Ottawa—came to visit. There weren't reliable home test kits in those days, and I didn't want to visit the doctor until after Judy left. I just wasn't drinking because the smell of my usual rum and cokes made me nauseated!

Yes, I understand now that should have been a clue.

The next years in Winnipeg passed happily enough with work, babies, a house, and friends. It had been city living, kind of, if just small city living. Movie theatres, restaurants, shopping malls. University for Don. A normal life starting a family, getting career promotions. I almost began to think about Winnipeg as my home town.

Almost. As usual, though, the military came calling. Still too young and rootless, we were tossed tumbling into the next posting. Cold Lake, Alberta. Back to a big Air Force Base in the middle of the northern Canadian scrublands, where screaming F-18s ruled the skies.

1991: WINNIPEG TO COLD LAKE. INTERMISSION.

*T*he good years had been upon us in Winnipeg. Although interest rates in 1987 were high, Great-West Life had offered employees mortgages at reduced rates, so before our second son was born, we bought a cute bungalow in River Heights, with tree-lined streets near the river, and walking distance across the bridge to the big Polo Park mall. No worries about the thirty year payments! Money was good: Don was an officer again, I was moving up at work. Then one day the inevitable.

❝ We're posted. To Cold Lake, Alberta."

We knew this day would come. Sell the house. Lose about fifteen grand on it; market was down. (There was no recourse from the military in 1991 for this.) So it was back to PMQs in Cold Lake, where I would be unemployed for almost a year waiting to finally get hired on a term-government-employee contract at DND, to work on base at the Weapons System Software Unit (WSSU). And where, about a year after I started, I would have to figure out how best to move on again. One year down, one year moving back up. We only had the two years in Cold Lake. I was just starting to like it when it was time to leave. But this time, when we left, it was with a personal victory achieved to ensure I wouldn't start from ground zero again.

The goal of every term employee with the Federal Government of Canada is to become a permanent employee. This is because permanent employees have more rights and privileges, according to their union contract, than term employees.

When a permanent employee competition opened up for my term position, I of course applied, even though such competitions took months to complete, and even though by the time of the position appointment, it was likely that Don would again be posted. Ah, but that was the point! If I won the competition, I would have the privilege of being a "spousal transfer" with DND, upon a move to a new posting. This would mean a job would await me next time, rather than having to start over again.

Here's how it all went down.

Lieutenant (Michele's boss): Michele, I hear your husband is posted!

Michele: How did you hear that?

Lieutenant: Hey, it's a small base. I know he's going to Ottawa.

Michele: I hope you don't think that will affect my application for the permanent CS02 competition that you're running.

Lieutenant: But . . . ? Aren't you moving? If you win the competition, how can you take the job? You're moving!

Michele: Well, just because my husband is posted, it doesn't have anything to do with my career, Lieutenant. In fact, if I don't get the position, I have to assume it is because you are discriminating against me because of my husband's situation. That would be illegal, right? That would be grounds for an appeal, right?

I won the competition.

Then we moved to Ottawa. As a permanent government employee, who moved because of my husband's military posting, I took advantage of the rules on priority placements, and had already set up a job in Ottawa that I had interviewed for over the phone.

The lieutenant wasn't mad. He put on a wonderful going-away lunch for me, and gave me a beautiful ceramic vase. Choked-up flashbacks to my childhood horse figurine collection overwhelmed me, and again, everyone at this going-away party was surprised I couldn't speak for whole moments at a time.

But finally, proudly, after a lifetime of bobbing around in the sea of camp-follower life, I'd acquired enough "motor skills" to power in my own direction. Little did I understand yet that pride is the greatest sin. There would be more lessons before my working days were settled, and my new powers of manipulation would be tested again.

*B*ut not yet, not until we left Cold Lake for Ottawa. In the *meantime, in Cold Lake I had started another part of my life, one that would define me for decades—that of "Hockey Mom." It would teach its own humbling lessons.*

1992: Cold Lake, Alberta. Hockey Mom Incident. (As told from 2010 Buffalo, New York.)

I like telling the story of my son's hockey beginnings as the proud older Hockey Mom I was when he accomplished his (and his parents') greatest hockey achievement: graduation from university. Believe me, not all hockey players at his level did. Pride is the greatest sin and I was no saint.

My future daughter-in-law Jessica and I are sitting on bleacher-style seats inside the stuffy auditorium. My husband Don is wandering the halls looking for fresh air while we wait for the commencement ceremony to begin. My son, D'Arcy, is graduating from Buffalo State College today. It's May, 2010, in Buffalo, New York. The flowers are in bloom, Jess and I are in cute little sun dresses, and I'm the happiest mom sweating here. Hard to believe where things come from.

Excited but bored and fidgety, Jessica has asked me about D'Arcy's early hockey life. Hockey is what got him recruited to Buff State, after his Triple A minor and then

Junior hockey careers. Jessica, his high-school sweetheart with whom he maintained his relationship over the years apart, stayed nearer to home and is about to graduate herself from Concordia University in Montréal. We're from Aylmer, Québec now, where Don and I settled for good after his retirement from the military two years ago in 2008 and where our boys call hometown.

Well, Jessica, I begin, you know we didn't move to Aylmer until D'Arcy was seven and already a veteran hockey star!

D'Arcy's first two years were played in Cold Lake, Alberta, where Don was a Logistics Officer in the Air Force and I worked as a computer programmer for WSSU, the Weapons Systems Software Unit. I love that name. I was only a civilian working on the Human Resource systems there, though; all the cool weapons stuff was done by the military software engineers, so don't blame me for any issues on the F-18s!

Anyway, D'Arcy was five, no, probably six that year, because his brother was already turning three, sneaking into the hockey gear bag and trying on equipment. One time we found him asleep on his little futon bed, wearing his big brother's helmet! That was a cute picture—I'll have to dig it up.

But here's a story for you. It was a Saturday morning, early and dark, and as usual, D'Arcy popped up from bed right away when I opened his door to wake him up. I wonder how hard I would have begged him if he hadn't been so darn eager—I would have killed to sleep in some Saturdays. I still sometimes wake up earlier on weekends than weekdays.

This particular Saturday, all was normal. Since it

had been Don's turn to stay home, it was just Mom and D'Arcy. The gear bag was packed by the door. We ate our TV dinners.

Yes, I know I told you this before, and you can't believe it, but we loved our microwaved chicken parmigiana dinners before hockey, yes, even at that hour. You've known D'Arcy long enough to know that at six years old, he'd have had no trouble putting a whole entree away and not puke it up on the ice an hour later!

Bundled up, out we went into the cold. I can't remember a morning that early in Cold Lake that wasn't frigid. D'Arcy carried his own gear bag to the back of the truck. Of course we had a truck—it was Alberta!

I know little kids today wear their gear to the rink, but we didn't dress them at home then. They changed at the rink in the dressing room, like the little men they were. I didn't go in the dressing room, though. I guess the coaches and other dads helped and tightened whatever needed doing.

So I unplug the truck, rev it up, and drive to the rink on tires that felt like blocks. It wasn't that far away as we lived on base there in Married Quarters, in PMQs. Yes, they were houses. I lived in them all my life but we always just called them PMQs, not houses.

We arrive at the rink; the sun is coming up now, a pink rosy sheen glowing on the shiny snow-packed pavement in the parking lot. D'Arcy hops out and around to the back to open the trunk gate and get the gear. Uh-oh. What? I run around to D'Arcy's little shriek.

You know he doesn't freak out easily. And we both just stand there in shock.

The gear bag was underneath the truck. *How is that*

possible? We dragged it out. It was shredded and hung up on the undercarriage. I must have backed over it in the driveway without putting it in the trunk! We look at each other and can't think of a word to say. *Did I usually put it in? D'Arcy was so independent and strong, did he usually do it?* Anyway, no one did it today. It had been dragged under the truck all the way there. We hauled and untangled what we could, and there was somewhat of a shell left to wrap everything in, so together we carted the ragged mess into the lobby of the rink and laid out the damage.

Incredibly, all the gear was there: helmet scraped; white plastic of the elbow pads intact, even though the straps are frayed, but nothing that hockey tape can't fix. Pants are dirty, but wearable. Skates? *Oh, please be okay*, I prayed. They had cost a fortune.

Yes, I know, he still insists on expensive skates. He always did!

And there they were, lying safely on one lace side each, precious blades in the air. I picked them up. The laces are shredded right off, the boots scuffed, but actually, they looked fine. I couldn't believe it. By now other kids were showing up so D'Arcy collected the remnants of the bag with his battered equipment and went to the dressing room. I bought new laces at the canteen and put them in and brought the skates to him just in time.

He played great. Yes, as usual!

Don tried to be upset with me later for driving over the bag, but really, he couldn't stop laughing long enough. I didn't think it was funny at the time.

Now look, Jessica, they're starting the ceremony and here comes Don. Yes, I do have a million of these hockey mom stories. I could write a book!

*A*nd I did, but I didn't tell many of the hockey-mom stories. Most are too painful to recollect. Cost. Injuries. Competition. God, the constant, brutal, insane, competition! I remember one of the boys getting cut from the team one year, and as we walked out of the rink, another mother—now, this woman was someone I'd shared rides with, eaten with at restaurants, sat and chatted with in hotels, in rink lobbies— well, she ran over and exclaimed, "Your son is cut? Oh, that's great! My son must've made the team then!" I can still see the sparkle in her eyes.

Let's put it this way: of all the years I spent doing time as "Hockey Mom," I kept pretty much zero of the "friends" from those days. That says something.

PART FOUR. ALL'S WELL that ENDS WELL.

1993: Ottawa, Ontario. House Hunting.

*W*e'd been two years at CFB Cold Lake (it was only just starting to be called 4 Wing then), and are now posted to National Defence Head Quarters (NDHQ) in Ottawa, Ontario. The capital of Canada, "The Big Posting", and potentially the final one in a logistics officer's career. We'd wiggled out of going east once before by accepting Cold Lake, trying to stay out west where we'd been since 1984 and closer to my parents in British Columbia, but Ottawa couldn't be avoided forever. So now, onto our first house-hunting trip!

We'll get a one week paid trip—travel time included—to Ottawa, to buy a house. Like in most big cities, there were not enough PMQs, so none are available to us in Ottawa, but that's okay. We've saved some money again and are eager to get to a city world, one where we can try out civilian life in an ordinary community, in an ordinary house.

The pre-trip meeting with a realtor liaison/advisor doesn't turn out to be very helpful but how could we have known then? We didn't know Ottawa at all. Luckily, many of my old college friends from Kingston days live there and my best friend Judy mails us newspapers with the real estate sections and a city map; this is still years before the Internet. Also, a friend from work knows the city and gives advice. Advice like, "No, you *won't be driving on Bank street for your daily commute, no matter what it looks like on the map." How right she turns out to be. Bank street is front and centre shops and rush-hour gridlock. As for the Québec side of the river, well, we are English, Anglophones, so the "advisor" doesn't even mention it. Again, what do we know? But we're excited, and this being 1993, it's a five-year-cycle "on" year for our high school reunion in Petawawa; we figure we can fit that weekend side trip in while having plenty of time to buy a house. All within five short days. What could be easier? It'll be like a vacation!*

Here's how the trip turned out.

❝Show me a house where I don't have to take this goddam' road to work every day!" Michele told the realtor. Her hands were still shaking as she put down her tea, sitting with her husband Don in the coffee shop where Mrs. Realtor had taken them after the car accident on the Queensway.

It was Thursday afternoon. The week-long house hunting trip was well underway. The Wednesday had been taken up with travel first to Edmonton, which itself was a four hour bus ride, then the military milk-run flight to Winnipeg, Trenton, and finally, Ottawa. They'd taken a taxi to arrive late at the downtown hotel, then had been up early to meet the realtor.

God, it's hot and humid in Ottawa in late May, thought Michele. She and Don were overdressed and feeling overstressed as they toured around looking at houses, and now . . .

Michele had been sitting up front with the agent in a big Lincoln Continental, or whatever it was, driving on that super highway they called the Queensway. Suddenly, right in front of them a zippy red Mazda had careened and fishtailed at high speed right into the sound barrier concrete wall on the right side of the road, clipping a couple of other cars along the way that then skidded and braked all over the lanes. Mrs. Realtor had hardly blinked, slowing carefully and pulling over to take out her brick of a 1990s car phone to call for help.

Michele meanwhile, former lifeguard training kicking in, had jumped out and raced ahead to the smashed-up red car, to cautiously peer into the rolled down driver's side window. To see a dark-haired ponytail flopped forward over the steering wheel between the clenched hands gripping it. No airbags, even on the driver's side.

The other young passenger leaned over to her friend and shook her while babbling, "Are you okay? Are you okay?"

Michele didn't have to worry. The shocked driver sat back up and started screaming incoherently, but obviously was not seriously hurt, and there was no blood. And now others including uniformed help was arriving, and Michele felt herself lifted off her feet and yanked backwards, back to the safety of the realtor's car by Don, who was swearing and furious that she'd run off so carelessly. Most of the cars screeching over to the far lanes away from the tangle were not even slowing down as they flew by.

So now, calmed somewhat by the sandwich and coffee break, the realtor showed them something in the Alta Vista neighbourhood, but it looked like a crack house, complete with numerous youths hanging in and around it, petting large mongrel dogs. Next was a nice single home in Beacon Hill that the couple couldn't afford, and finally they went to Blackburn Hamlet to see a townhouse, which wasn't too bad. A bit small, but move-in ready. Growing up as base kids, Michele and Don had never learned to be handy around the house, so "no fixer-uppers, please." The realtor was desperate to show them something in Orleans; she said it was where most of the military in Ottawa lived. But if they couldn't live on base, Michele and Don didn't want to live in the fake "CFB" Orleans, as it was nicknamed. They were eager to live in the real world and raise their boys there. They firmly resisted going to Orleans.

It grew late. Time to go out for a nice dinner in the touristy Market area then get ready for the weekend in Petawawa. They told the realtor they'd call her back Sunday night. Over dinner they figured they'd probably have to make an offer on the Beacon Hill townhouse.

In the rental car on Friday, which was red like the accident car, Michele and Don decided to head for Pembroke and Petawawa through the Québec side; Michele was still shaky about the Queensway. After an easy bridge crossing against the morning commute traffic and as soon as they turned left onto Upper Aylmer Road, the contrast from the sweaty concrete of downtown Ottawa was remarkable. Fluorescent spring-green on budding maples lined the lush golf holes just visible beyond the road. There was calm two-lane traffic. The air was fresher, not city sticky, and as the day warmed, they turned off the car radio and rolled down the windows. The soft scent of lilacs washed past. The rush of the big city just across the bridge seemed a world away.

Aylmer proper quaintly announced itself with a hand-painted billboard picturing an old-time carriage pulled by horses, that read, "Calmez vos chevaux. Vous arrivez en ville." Charming! Michele was loving the ambience of Aylmer. She grew excited to practice her high-school French. They stopped just after the sign at the McDonald's. (In later years, they would call this same McDonald's "McDo," like locals did.)

After their McMuffins and juice, they turned the red rental car into the neighbourhood behind the shopping mall. Ahead of schedule, they decided to look around. They soon deciphered that "Maison à vendre" was the sign to look for, and not "Vendu," meaning "Sold." They wrote down some addresses to check out on Monday. There were cozy family homes for sale, in neighbourhoods with playgrounds and schools. Clean streets. Lovely!

It was a clear sunny day, and Don and Michele headed for Petawawa on the country road Route 148 in a much improved state of mind. They were ready for the vacation part of this tour: to go back in time to party up the weekend with their high school friends, which they had done every five years since leaving Petawawa. How wonderful that they'd made it again this year!

Tired but refreshed when they drove back on Sunday afternoon, they checked out Aylmer again and it still seemed perfect for their family. Shopping mall, walkable neighbourhoods, a hockey rink not far away, schools, ball diamonds, playgrounds. By the time they drove back to downtown Ottawa to their hotel, they were eager to call Mrs. Realtor.

"Sorry, I can't show you anything for sale in Québec. Out of province," she said when Michele started to give her addresses they wanted to see. "Are you sure you want to live over there? Do you even speak French?"

This seemed a little rude. Although not bilingual,

Michele and Don were not afraid of French. Michele insisted they wanted to look in Aylmer. So the realtor lady, finally behaving professionally, called her contact in Gatineau, and Don and Michele met him at the Aylmer McDonald's first thing Monday morning. Their week was ticking away to the Wednesday departure. They had to find something today!

The first house they looked at was a stand-alone two-storey with attached garage on the winding street behind the McDonald's, walking distance to the mall and main road with its bus stops. There was a playground in a kiddie park not far either. It had three bedrooms, a powder room on the main floor, although the bathroom fixtures were blue. It had a dated finished basement with wood panelling, but it was still a nice family room. The back yard had a big deck, and privacy with cedar hedges. All in all perfect for their young family.

"How much?" It seemed ridiculous when the realtor said, $99,900. A similar house they'd seen in Ottawa had been over $150,000, and it didn't even have a finished basement.

"Why so low? What's wrong with it?" they asked.

"No, nothing wrong. C'est juste le prix." The realtor consulted his papers again and shrugged.

Michele and Don found out later he was from Gatineau proper, and didn't know the Aylmer sector that well. He thought the price was high, not low. Aylmer to the west had always been pricier than the eastern side of the someday-to-be-amalgamated city of Gatineau. And of course real estate was at least 30 percent cheaper on this side of the river from Ottawa, but Michele and Don wouldn't have known that yet. Smelling a sucker military sale, Monsieur le Realtor kept this knowledge and his opinion of fair prices to himself.

"It seems too good to be true, so let's look at some more?"

They spent the rest of the day looking at some more, but none compared with that first house, so at around 4:00 p.m. they sat down and filled out the offer.

"We'd like to offer 99," said Michele, "but need to hear back from them by 6:00 p.m. If we buy it, we have to go to the bank tomorrow and finalize everything. And then we leave on Wednesday. What do you think? Will that be an okay offer?"

"I don't know how they could refuse such a generous offer. I will call you at the hotel, yes? Around six."

The call wasn't late. "Of course they accept," Monsieur said, "But no, not for July. September after the long weekend at the earliest for your possession."

What could they do? They had to agree. It meant Don would have to go to Ottawa for work in July by himself while Michele and the kids would follow at the end of August, for their oldest son to start school. School started in Québec the last week of August.

D'Arcy didn't know it then, but starting a new school from a hotel room would be his last real base-brat experience, because Aylmer would become his hometown. Don would take four or five postings in Ottawa to keep the family there, giving up on promoting his career, and then would retire there, too. A hometown for the kids, and now the adopted home of Michele and Don.

*W*ho knew? We certainly didn't think in 1993 that we'd retire in Québec. My parents and other relatives all lived out west. One of my three brothers would eventually also retire from the military and stay in Ottawa, but the other two ended up with one in Victoria, British Columbia, and the other in Edmonton, Alberta. Many military siblings are spread across the country as adults; the distances meant we never kept in close contact. It was—is—sad, but it's a fact of our existence, and accepted as a consequence of our lifestyle.

Meanwhile, the die was cast. Our two sons would have a hometown: Aylmer, Québec.

And through no real skill on our part, Don and I finally had outlasted the youthful years of sucker buys of cars and houses. We moved four times in Aylmer, each one a success after losing somewhat on that first, overpriced one. Of course we only bought new cars after the Omega, so there were no longer any issues there, either. The boys would have a great hometown, complete with good schools, sports and friends. Can't complain about some good luck on a move for a change!

1993-2008: The Immigrant Years

*S*o, *we could have moved to Ottawa in Ontario, but we chose Aylmer. We'd been out west for a decade, and these were the years when the political rulers of Québec were the Parti Québecois. As fiercely proud Canadians, of course we knew that the PQ wanted to establish their own country of Québec, separate from the ROC, that is, the rest of Canada. Our family and friends couldn't understand why we wanted to live on that side of the river.*

As mentioned, housing was less expensive. Aylmer was closer to the downtown Federal public service buildings—which employed most of the National Capital Region—than the more expensive Ontario suburbs of Orleans or Kanata. Commutes were shorter, bus passes were cheaper, and so was daycare. Daycare wasn't as cheap as it would get after my kids were too old to take advantage of it, but it was still not as pricey as in Ontario.

Aside from the cost of living: I didn't realize it at the time, but should have guessed based on my own experiences growing up—the school system in Québec seemed stronger than Ontario, especially in math and the sciences. Ontario still struggled in those days with that grade thirteen problem, too.

Because it was less populated on the Québec side of the river, it was, to me, immediately more beautiful once over the bridge. The road to Aylmer was lined along the river with golf courses, and the town itself was old enough to have its own character with blocky limestone buildings and a public square dominated by century-old trees. A suburb of Ottawa, yes, despite being in Québec, Aylmer nevertheless has always been its own town.

The question wasn't why did we settle in *la belle province,* but why didn't everyone? And so we come to it, the reason for the population disparity. The language issue. French.

I can admit now that we were drawn to Québec for the thrill of living somewhere different—to experience another culture, another language, to enjoy living in a new province. We were both base brats, Don and I, and used to the changes of life that each move would bring. I guess we were looking forward to the excitement of the unknown.

We were still young. We had two young boys. D'Arcy had already done kindergarten and grade one in French Immersion in Cold Lake. My own dream of being bilingual could be allowed another chance, and also be transferred to the children, as many under-achieved goals of parents are. I remember how positively I pushed the second language idea to my son D'Arcy when he was turning five in Cold Lake. Every time *Sesame Street* would do a French-language spot on their TV show, I'd remind D'Arcy to pay attention because he was going to go to French immersion.

Me: D'Arcy, how exciting that you're starting kindergarten!

In French! By the way, are you sure you want to go to French kindergarten instead of English?

D'Arcy: Oh yes, mom! Of course!

Me: Why not English kindergarten?

D'Arcy: Because I don't know what English is!

Okay, maybe I oversold it. . .

Anyway, we did buy our house in Québec. And if the aim was to have an interesting experience, well, the language issues did ensure that.

In grade two:

D'Arcy: Mom, we learned about phoque today in school!

Hmm . . . pronounced like a bad F-word in English.

Me: Really? And what is that?

D'Arcy: A phoque is a seal. I like phoques, ha-ha, I like phoques!

Me: Very amusing. I get it. Okay, that's enough.

D'Arcy: Ha-ha, phoque, phoque, phoque . . .

Our younger son Sasha was only three when we moved to Aylmer, so we put him in a daycare near D'Arcy's school. The teachers were young and nice and always spoke their adorable accented English to us. Kindergarten for four year-olds was just starting when Sasha turned four, and after discussion with the daycare teachers, we agreed they provided the same kind of K-4 program right there, so no need to bus to the separate "real" school for a few hours a day. Sasha was a chatty, agreeable child, and had no problems at the daycare, or with their K-4-like curriculum. The next year, at five years-old, he moved up to the French Immersion program in the English school board system that his brother was already in.

On meeting his kindergarten teacher:

Me: Nice to meet you! Sasha says you're a nice teacher. He really likes it here at school.

Teacher: Oh, you're English. So it must be Sasha's father who is the Francophone.

Me: What? No. Why do you say that?

Teacher: Then why is Sasha a Francophone?

I look at Sasha, sitting innocently with me at the parent-teacher interview.

Me: Sasha, can you speak French?

Sasha: Yes, mom, of course.

At that moment I realized that the daycare he'd been in for two years had been a French daycare. The parents are always the last to know. Truthfully, I'd never thought to ask.

A similar thing happened with D'Arcy's first summer job, at sixteen, which he got at a nearby golf course. He'd just returned from his interview:

Me: Well, how did the interview go?

D'Arcy: Great! I got the job!

Me: That's wonderful! Congratulations! What did they ask you?

D'Arcy: If I could drive, did I mind cleaning washrooms, you know, regular stuff. Oh, after he said he needed me to start this weekend, he said that oh, by the way, they had lots of English customers and . . . could I speak English?

Me: You mean, the interview was all in French?

D'Arcy: Yes, of course, mom. He was happy that I told him, yes, I could speak English.

So, a mom's dream realized. My kids even had the full Outaouais accent that passed for native. Well, because they were native, I realized. It was the parents who were the "immigrants." Although we both had learned enough

French to get by in the province, we never would achieve the kind of bilingualism that the children had. First, we were too old to ever get that fluent, and second, because Aylmer was the most bilingual place I'd ever been; people were just too nice to us Anglo immigrants!

An example:

Grocery clerk: Papier ou plastique, Madame?

Me: N'importe quel. Okay, plastique.

Clerk: That'll be $14.95, please.

Me: Why did you switch to English? Is my French so bad?

Clerk: Oh, no, sorry! I'm English too, is all!

Maybe she was, but I couldn't tell from *her* accent. Like she could with mine.

The real test of our transplanted Anglophone lives was the October referendum, 1995, when the ruling Parti Québecois asked its citizens to vote on becoming a country separate from the rest of Canada. It was on our nineteenth wedding anniversary, no less. I can't remember where we went out for lunch to celebrate that day, but I know we hadn't been apart for a single anniversary ever; we always made sure to go out at least for lunch, if not supper. Not many supper anniversaries on Mondays when the kids were little, though. So did we take the day off work and meet up for lunch? Just grab a quick lunch together at work that day? I can't remember.

What I do remember of that time was that we had two young boys, it was a Monday, and as D'Arcy was only nine years old, we would have had to pick him up from after-school daycare, then go to the other school where Sasha was in kindergarten and get him, too. Did we vote before or after we picked up the kids? Again, I've no recollection at all. Probably after. We liked to take the boys with us on after-work errands.

We would have had supper, something quick to make, like a "mush," which was pasta or rice mixed with frozen veggies and ground pork stirred together with a mushroom soup or spaghetti sauce. Then the normal routine would have been to help D'Arcy with early-week homework, before the later-week hockey practices would interfere. We would have watched some TV, the kids would have had baths, then reading time before bed. I know we had early bedtimes: these were the busy working years. The boys were good sleepers and went to bed at the same time together to read; although the house had three bedrooms, they shared a room with bunk beds. When we sold the house years later, I found doodles in marker on the wall under the bottom bunk. I guess Sasha was more of an artist than reader at that age.

Hectic day done, curled together with a comforter on the futon, Don and I settled downstairs in our basement family room to watch the referendum results. And almost died of shock at the eight o'clock announcement that the Yes vote—to separate—was leading. Québec was voting to separate from Canada.

Now, we did not expect this. Aylmer was a Federal Government suburb; most people worked downtown Ottawa. There had been lots of Yes signs up all over the Outaouais during the campaign, sure, especially around Université de Hull, and of course, more of them the further east into Gatineau. People chatted about it at the rink, and at work it was a big topic of conversation, especially with the Ottawa-side co-workers who demanded to know what we English Quebeckers would do if we separated—did we think Canada would just take us in, like refugees? There was anger in the ROC about Québec rejecting them. But separation was an unreal scenario for me; I didn't give it much credence. As a proud and lifelong Canadian first, it was a no-brainer for me, and I guess I assumed it would be for most other voters. We'd only been in Québec for two years. We owned our house, but figured the military would bail us out in any unimaginable scenario. Don was adamant that he wouldn't heed the PQ call to cross over to any new Québec country's military. We had joked about it, but never thought anything like these worst-case scenarios would play out.

And now here was Peter Mansbridge on CBC telling us that yes, the separation vote was leading. I guess we were going to get more of an exciting life in Québec than we'd ever dreamed possible!

Don and I sat unmoving and not talking much about it for the next couple of hours. But finally the West-end Montréal votes started coming in, late. To tip the No side to a slim victory. Later, we would hear rumours that many, many No votes had been suspiciously spoiled, but no matter now.

Canada was intact and still included Québec.

Curiously, people I knew in Aylmer hardly talked about separation or the fallout from the close vote. English and French—and many families were both—we all just carried on, living life, raising kids, working, going to kids' hockey games.

But it was a turnaround moment for us, and Don and I decided shortly after that night to move up to a nicer house, one that we would have built for us, on a big park down by the river, beside an outdoor rink and soccer field, where our boys could have an active childhood. Where we would never discuss again the possibility of leaving Aylmer, or Québec.

*B*y 2008, when Don retired from the military and we had one last chance to give up on "la belle province" with a paid military move, we didn't. We couldn't. Our kids were from Aylmer now. And like immigrants everywhere, after so many years, without realizing when it had happened, we belonged here now, too.

Besides, where else would we go?

1993: Public Servant

Although I have changed names and allowed fill-ins for memory, this is the story of my first job in Ottawa. It could be called "The Way She Learned How Things Work in the Public Service." Another lesson on watching your back, that's for sure. It was a pivotal moment in my career—things could certainly have turned out worse!

Michele couldn't decide if her boss was joking or not. She smiled awkwardly.

"Really, Wilson?" she asked. "You think there are people who would spy on your computer screen through the window? From there?"

"There" was the boulevard outside, not busy except at rush hour. Back then the open, empty quarry across the street lay dormant, zoned for a casino someday in downtown Hull. Wilson kept the blinds closed to the sweeping seventh-floor view, even on a gloriously sunny, winter day like today.

"Michele, I've told you before, yes, there are spies in Ottawa who would love to telescope the secret DND information I have on my screen. Don't ask me to open the blinds again," he said patiently, but with that deriding undertone, patronizing.

So, not joking then. Michele retreated to her cubicle and unlocked the combination on the filing cabinet where more codes for the hardware room were kept. Wilson made her change the combination weekly, and she was supposed to memorize it for her daily access. Blushing, she recalled the first time Wilson had told her the combination—and received the blistering reprimand to go to the orderly room and have the pad of paper she'd written it on, shredded, because of course someone could use a pencil to shade over the imprints to see the numbers. At least the sergeant at the desk had laughed when she explained what Wilson had ordered and muttered something conspiratorial about what a jackass he was.

It was almost 3:30 p.m. and time to change the overnight tapes before she left for the day. A routine government IT job, even if just a term position. As a spousal transfer to Ottawa from Cold Lake with her military husband, she'd accepted this job over the phone. Wilson had seemed happy to hire her, explaining that the two-year term was just a formality, and that she could expect to maybe take over from him after he'd won one of the competitions he was applying for. Michele was becoming more eager to help Wilson achieve his goal. Lately, she'd begun exploring her own options. As a database administrator with server experience and programming background, she could have her pick of positions in a government town.

"Goodnight, Michele," waved the sergeant at the reception desk where Michele locked up the previous night's backups.

"Thanks, Sergeant! See you tomorrow." She double-yanked the handle on the cabinet. *Locked and loaded,* she grinned in her head, *until tomorrow.*

But the next day, Friday, Michele called in sick to go on a school outing with her son. Wilson wouldn't have pre-approved it, she knew. She left a message on his phone.

Spring was definitely coming. Michele was writing documentation one day, when Wilson appeared over her, form quivering in his hands.

"Michele, you have a security violation, from the military police checks on the weekend."

What? Harsh, but Wilson seems nervous, she thought. Michele looked up at him, but he didn't offer the paper for her to see.

"You're supposed to lock the filing cabinet by the orderly room every night, right?"

"Well, yes, and I always do. Every single night."

"Oh good, you admit it was you. Okay, don't worry, this will be a first offence, and you'll keep your clearance. As long as you admit it, no problem. Good." He ran off.

Michele closed up her document on the screen and walked to the orderly room to look at job postings, not caring if Wilson saw her.

The next day an MP and Wilson's boss, the major, asked her to join them in a boardroom. They wanted her to sign something, it was an official warning, after two years clear of further incidents, it would be expunged, that any other infractions would be permanently on her record, which could lead to a possible revocation of Secret-level, blah, blah, blah.

Dizzy, Michele asked to see the paper. The date was from the month before, not this past weekend.

"I never leave the cabinet unlocked. This is dated last month. Wilson said it was on the weekend."

"Yes, but you must have left it unlocked on the Friday before this Sunday check," the MP said.

The major didn't say anything.

"But I was sick one Friday last month, and I keep my leave passes and this is the weekend after my Friday off, I'm sure. I can go get the pass, to show you."

"Who unlocks in the morning and locks up when you're not here?"

Michele looked at the major. "Wilson is the only other person I know who does, to do the daily tape changes."

The major still didn't say anything.

"So, I'm not signing anything," Michele said, and the two men let her leave, saying they would investigate further.

"Why did you tell the MPs I left the cabinet unlocked?" Wilson appeared over her desk, head lowered to hers.

"I didn't. I said that it wasn't me, that's all."

"Well, you and I are the only ones with the combination, so you basically said it was me!"

"I didn't say it was you. I said it wasn't me."

Wilson straightened. And ran off.

Michele was let go at the end of fiscal year, "due to departmental cutbacks." The sergeant confirmed that "Michele always locked the cabinet, every night", and the MPs closed the violation as "unresolved." The major signed expenses for Wilson for the security conference, knowing Wilson must have returned the classified material to the office, to lock in the cabinet, sometime during the weekend before the Sunday in question, so as not to take it to his home, which would have been a violation. And Wilson could not afford another violation.

Wilson won a competition and moved up in the

government. He eventually became a Chief Information Security Officer.

Michele never had a violation. She quit her public service position to become a consultant where in a government town like Ottawa, she made more money, even more than the major or a CISO, in her long, careful career.

The major retired, tired.

I don't really know if the major retired, but probably. And I'm sure he was tired!

I left my permanent public service position in 1997 to work as an independent consultant. Meaning I did the exact same work as the public servants I worked alongside with in my contracts with the Federal Government, but didn't have their benefits or job security. Just a higher salary. And less politics, thank God! Life is trade-offs, and I was happy with my choice. I'd learned not just the lessons I needed to succeed in my career, but how to apply them. I would stand up for myself from here on in.

Raising Boys

*H*ockey *Mom. I even had the button.*
   New co-worker: So, you're a consultant? You must be rich.
   Me: Well, I do have two boys in competitive hockey to support.
   Co-worker: Oh, sorry, then you must be broke!

I did know some parents who calculated the yearly costs of the hockey-parenting life, but I never did. I didn't want to know. We made enough money for a nice house, two cars, and to pay for the yearly leather team jackets. I wouldn't go with Don to buy the boys their skates. I think they wore the same brands and models as professional NHL players, plus they needed a new size every year— sometimes a new size within a year. No hand-me-downs, either, as D'Arcy was magnificently brutal on footwear; we were lucky if one pair made it through the season. Same for sticks! You wouldn't believe what those fancy composite sticks cost when they first came out. Like about other costs, I never wanted to know exactly how many they used per season. Quite ridiculous. But we did it.

And when the boys both went to the States—D'Arcy to university in Buffalo the same year Sasha left for his last two years of high school to attend a prestigious Prep school near Boston—we continued to support them and pay most costs, even though they both had hockey "deals" with their expensive American schools. Not to mention all the travelling we did in those years to keep up with them, driving from Ottawa to Boston or Buffalo every second weekend or so. Hotels, school costs, car costs: I refuse to speculate what the total must have been! Considerable, I guess.

The rationale? Unlike their parents, our boys had grown up in one place, their hometown. No uprooting for them, but also not seeing much of the world. Their childhoods had been as different from ours as ours had been from our parents', which is probably true of every generation, it seems to me now. But hockey allowed them opportunities to get out and experience a little more of that wider world, like their parents had had growing up. We knew we could help to make that happen, and that's what we did.

I don't begrudge the costs of raising kids, nor the extra, extra costs of their sports, nor even the extra, extra, extra costs of their schooling in "Americaland."

What's money for, if not to build better lives for the children? Is this attitude a reflection of our base-kid upbringings, those of Don and myself? It didn't hurt that we were used to the sacrifices one makes for the greater good, and if that's a stretch, (I know plenty of people who sacrificed for their kids) well, that's my story and I'm sticking to it.

2001: Saint Somewhere near Montréal

*B*ecause the boys both played top-level competitive hockey growing up in Aylmer, Québec, it meant their leagues were mostly in Montréal and environs. Due to interprovincial restrictions we couldn't stay in the Ottawa leagues so the closest other team would be at least two hours' drive away. Don and I would split up each weekend, one each with one son. The incident below was typical of my taking Sasha to "Saint Somewhere sur Some River or another," near Montréal on a Saturday or Sunday afternoon. The details all happened, but some on some days, some at other times.

*A*rrival at the away town's rink, the requisite two hours ahead of game time: some parents will sit in the lobby and gossip while drinking Timmie's, if the town has a Tim Horton's, or arena hot chocolate, if not. No one ever drinks what was called coffee from the arena. Others leave after dropping their son off to pick up groceries or get gas, and some sit in their cars reading or napping.

Michele wanders and paces around the lobby. She doesn't like going for walks by herself in these circuitous, unknown neighbourhoods where the hockey arenas were inevitably nestled. Manon, Michele's friend, shows up late with her son Jean-Michel, but still within the coach's strict timeline. Boys, unrecognizable without their gear and numbers, run past them in the lobby in ripe-smelling T-shirts and shorts or long johns emblazoned with *UnderArmour,* to do laps in the parking lot for warm-ups. Finally, game time approaches. The Zamboni does its last licking loop and leaves the ice, the engine roar cutting out suddenly to the loud slam of the gates behind it. Parents grab a fresh hot chocolate and go through the swinging heavy doors, out into the stands.

"Manon, the home team's moms are sitting on this side. Let's go over there." Michele points down to the wooden stands by the other blue line.

The rink is filling in with the usual assortment of hockey parents: dads in dark team jackets and ball caps, the moms as stylish as possible in parkas and boots and lipstick. Michele is holding her blanket to sit on. This rink had overhead gas heaters, but you couldn't count on getting a seat under one. Besides, they burned your head while your feet froze.

"*Mais, non!* The sign it say, 'Visiteur,' behind here, *ici.* What is wrong with them those moms? Do they not know which stupid side to sit in their own rink?" Loud and well-known for her trash-talking the other teams, Manon firmly holds her place.

"But Manon, our team moms are showing up and going over there. *Allons-y,* okay? Let's go!"

Michele and Manon often share rides with the boys on these weekend day trips to somewhere around Montréal. The towns had unpronounceable French names starting with *St.* or *Ste.*, depending on the particular male or female saint they were named for. Their boys are hockey friends—they'd played together since they were four, in Aylmer, until aged ten when they'd both made the big team, *L'Intrépide*, which represented the Outaouais region in the Québec league. Today, though, Manon and her son Jean-Michel had to go home a different way to meet up with another hockey brother playing nearby, so Michele and Sasha had found the big old barn-style rink in this snowy little town themselves. No GPS or Google Maps back then. They would plan the route the old-fashioned way ahead of time, then Sasha, at eleven, would navigate. He was near-sighted enough to read the well-worn map book in the car, and in fact was better at it than Michele.

Now the home team moms arrive, glaring, and move in right beside Manon. Despite her exaggerated look at the sign, and complaining all the while, she got up and joined Michele to move down to the other end of the stands. This rink only had seating on the one side of the rink, hence the need for the sign for which side would sit where, which the home town parents ignored anyway.

Finally, they all settle in for the game—*le match*. Goalie Dad positions himself at the opposite end zone, to pace and switch ends in between periods. Manon sits with plenty of space around her. Most of the other moms are cliques from Gatineau or Hull, and besides, Michele is the rare other mom who can handle listening to Manon's verbal assaults on the referees. Probably because Michele is Anglophone and doesn't understand how vile some of the insults are in French. One time a referee had skated over to the boards and warned Manon that further abuse would get her ejected from the rink, but this was years before hockey parents had to sign any contracts promising good behaviour, and of course neither the referees had followed up with their threats, nor had Manon quieted down.

Now the warmup begins: two teams worth of excited boys whipping around their zones, skate blades ripping and shredding as they carve the corners, stirring a breeze of the last wisps of Zamboni diesel into the stands. Echoes boom from their newly-developed slap-shots slamming on the boards. This rink is old enough to still have the high cathedral roof and intricate wood construction. Awesomely impressive. Exceptionally cold. The boys go to their benches, the referee blows his whistle, the teams face off. Gametime: always thrilling for Michele and Manon.

Jean-Michel and Sasha are assistant captains. As ranking (only) Anglophone on the team, Sasha is often needed to speak to referees or other coaches who can't speak French. Not the case here today, though. St. Somewhere is typically unilingual Francophone. The visiting parents had already guessed, correctly, that these referees would be homers. All the small-town refs were, especially against the *Outaouais Intrépide,* who had an unfair reputation for being too rough. Really they were just a good team, always at the top of the league and often champions, year after year. They had a large pool of players to pull from: the entire Outaouais from Shawville, west of Aylmer, to Papineauville and Maniwaki to the east and north. They played a lot of Ontario tournaments, separated only by the river from Ottawa, so their style was noticeably different from the rest of their league. Perhaps more physical. But in Ontario, their reputation was that of speedy little Frenchmen!

"*Tabernouche!* Another penalty for us—*rudesse*—for Jean-Michel," Manon mumbles with distress.

The game is tied. Some other mothers titter and glance at Manon. Snidely, they know if they are scored against now, it is likely Jean-Michel will be benched a shift or two, meaning better ice time for their own boys. And ice time is the name of the game at this competitive level. Michele knew of one mother once who actually carried a stop-watch and notepad. What she did with it, Michele couldn't imagine; complaints to the coach never ended well. She recalled another mother who had complained about a punishment practice last year—you know, after a bad game, when the kids are skated and skated to exhaustion doing lines, circles, laps. She'd said she was a doctor and that this kind of physical exertion wasn't right for ten year olds. The coaches agreed it wasn't right for *her* ten year old. There had been less ice time for him from that point, and he didn't make the cut the following year.

Now this year, at age eleven, body checking is not yet technically allowed, and the homer referees would call any incidental contact by the visitors with a two-minute roughing penalty. Michele leans forward, eager to see who would be put out on this penalty kill. Sasha has good anticipation and puck control; he often gets the shift. He likes the chance to score short-handed, when hogging the puck is not discouraged by the coaches with benched shifts.

And yes, in a close game like this, here he comes to take the face-off in their zone. Low and back-handed, Sasha scoops the puck behind his net to his defenceman, while breaking up the right wing, awaiting then receiving the expected pass up. And now he fakes into the middle, crossing up the opposing white-sweatered winger who sweeps desperately back at him with his stick. Too late, though. Sasha accelerates up the boards, cuts in around the defenceman over their blue line, and glances up in preparation for a snap on goal, but slides it across to his teammate following up the middle instead. Who one-times it towards the center of the net, now unprotected as the goalie is still set up for the shot from the right. Score!

Another win for the *Intrépide*. Another away weekend afternoon ending. The other parents leave quickly, the boys tromping out bent over with gear bags almost as big as themselves hunched over their backs. It is getting dark outside and smells like snow. Manon waves goodbye as she follows Jean-Michel out of the rink.

Michele waits for Sasha. He's always slow out of the dressing room. A dawdler and chatterbox, he waits until last for the shower so he can take longer. The coaches have even left now, nodding but not stopping to speak to parents on the way out. Michele is the last one left.

The lights in the lobby start to go out so she shouts down the hallway to the dressing rooms, "Hey, wait, attendez s'il vous plaît! Mon gars n'est pas encore sortie!" *Where in the hell is Sasha? He hasn't come out yet. Is there another exit?*

The rink attendant flicks the lights back on with a scowl at Michele's bad accent, and just as she's about to go to the room herself, out comes Sasha, bag humped over his back, shirt open and tie un-done, hair a wet mess. One hand carries his sticks, the other, clutched close to his body, holds in a neck-guard, some headphones, and another tie.

"Some guys forgot their stuff," he says with a grin, face shiny and happy. As last one out, he does cleanup duty.

"Well, come on, I can't remember how to get out of here and it's getting dark. Do you have your homework to do in the car?"

"Yup, sure. Can we stop for a bagel at Tim Horton's? I got the winning assist."

"I know, I saw."

They listen to a *Linkin' Park* CD and sing on the drive all the way home.

*T*here were some good times being hockey mom, I have to admit.

2003: Junior Hockey

The boys were known as playmakers and goal-scorers, but Junior Hockey also included hockey fights, stories about which mother this author could hardly bear to listen to, much less watch. This story is a creative conglomeration of a couple of those fights that happened as described by D'Arcy.

The home-team forward grinned crookedly at the rookie winger lined up against him on the faceoff. D'Arcy replied with a quizzical look back. He could see right away that this guy was the enforcer. He must be six-three at least, and his grey jersey was snug around the middle. He was almost albino pale, but had deep, black eyes and white-blond brush-like bearded growth showing under the regulation visor. No facemask. The crowd had started chanting "Fight! Fight!" when he stepped on the ice—his first shift of the game and it was already the third period.

So D'Arcy was wary when the big guy crossed his stick over his and said, "Wanna go?"

Now D'Arcy knew he should ignore the brute. His visiting team was winning by a goal, and it was late in the third period. Coach was strict about the job out here now: set things up, control the puck, don't do anything stupid to lose this game. D'Arcy was still a rookie and it wouldn't take too many mistakes to put him on the bench or even out of the lineup for the next game. His role was playmaker, not fighter.

But hey, he's seventeen, big and strong himself, and can't resist.

"Sure," he shrugged, and as he ripped at his helmet, a screw on the front of it where his facemask was attached gouged deep into his forehead. The sight of D'Arcy's face streaming blood and sweat froze Goon-boy just long enough—D'Arcy got a lucky first swing. Then down they went in the classic player embrace, rolling and tousling and intertwining with the referees who had joined the tangle. Pulled apart, getting up panting and drained, they're both grinning now!

Penalties all around, towels in the box bloodied and wet; the fight had energized the home crowd, and then the home team.

After the loss, D'Arcy's coach grabbed the manager: "I told you, we need our own enforcer, I can't afford to have goal-scoring rookies get killed out there!"

*B*ut D'Arcy was lucky, and he never got really hurt in his *few fights. Even better, no one called him out to do the "player dance" too much after that, nor for the rest of his Junior career. He does still have the scar in his forehead from the screw gouge.*

I sometimes think we hockey parents should've been arrested for child abuse, putting our kids in such a sport! But they loved it, and certainly after puberty we couldn't control their own choices about where and when to play. We continued to support them, through fun and tough times alike. In fact, I consider myself a successful hockey mom because my boys did love their sport and today, after College and Junior hockey, they continue to play for fun, as adults. Mom sometimes goes out to watch, but not too often. The beer leagues have kind of late ice times. Let the new, young hockey wives do their own duty!

2012: THE LAST CONTRACT

After my time as a Computer Programmer Analyst, then Database Administrator in the Public Service, I became an information technology (IT) consultant, where in Ottawa, I would never be unemployed. Consultants were independent but got their government contracts through agencies which won bids through competitive processes. I would receive a contract offer from an agency at a certain daily rate of pay known as a per diem, and could negotiate for more, then take it or leave it. I did pretty well. This episode shows just how well I did end up.

You know you've made it when . . .

"I have a contract renewal for the both of you," Kent, our contract agent, said. "But I had to bid the two of you at the same per diem. I've worked it out that neither of you will get a decrease but one of you is stuck at their same old rate while I got to pull the other one's rate up to match it. Are you both okay with this?"

Since I was the newer consultant at the department, and a woman, I assumed that my male co-worker and the longer-term consultant, Frank, would naturally have had the higher of our original rates. So eagerly, stupidly, of course I agreed.

"Good, I'm happy you agree, Michele, because Frank, now you will be getting the higher rate that Michele is already earning."

2013: THE LAST MOVE

*L*et's start with a flashback:
Me: Grandma, I'm expecting!
Grandma: How nice, I hope you have a boy!
Me: Why?
Grandma: Because all men need boys.

*A*few years later, after my first boy:
Me: Grandma, I'm expecting my second one!
Grandma: Wonderful—I hope you have a girl!
Me: But why, Grandma, I thought you wanted me to have boys?
Grandma: No, just the first. You need a girl for you. Boys will leave you someday, so you need a daughter to look after you later.

*I*had another boy. So I prayed for good daughters-in-law!

Jessica turned to her mother-in-law, her gigantic plaid scarf piled around rosy cheeks against the sharp early December wind blowing on the hill, and said, "You know,

Michele, I think it's a good idea. Hey, at least once a year someone will put a wreath on your grave!"

Michele looked back at her pretty blond daughter-in-law, at a loss for how to respond. She adored her, but sometimes wondered if Jessica could be a little heartless, like now, suggesting that her in-laws needed to buy their burial plot. What did she mean? Still speechless, Michele took in the sight of her family mingling around the military headstones at the Beechwood Cemetery in Ottawa. She looked at her husband Don, bending over to read an inscription, at her grown sons D'Arcy and Sasha talking together and pointing, and of course back to Jessica, D'Arcy's wife of over a year now. After an organized ceremony called *Wreathes Across Canada*, they'd all just finished placing evergreen boughs with bright red ribbons on gravestones for resting veterans, and had lingered to browse and reflect. The day was harsh and steel-cold, but they all felt cheered looking at the green and crimson splashes those wreaths made on the otherwise colourless uniformity of the countless stone markers.

True, Michele had just casually commented to Jessica, "You know, Jess, Don and I are eligible to buy a plot and be buried here, like this, in the National Military Cemetery, due to his thirty-plus years in the Air Force." It had been just a passing remark, and Jessica's serious reply had caught her off-guard.

"Yes, but we're not planning on needing this anytime soon, Jess!" Michele continued, maybe a little crisply, then softening, added, "But you're right, I just never really thought about it until this minute."

Michele and Don were only in their fifties, both healthy, with duties and jobs almost finished. Sasha was still living at home, on and off, as he sputtered and started to launch his own life of responsibilities, but he wouldn't take long to get going; eventually he would join the military himself. D'Arcy and Jess were both working and had just bought their first home. Michele was waiting for grandchildren, for heaven's sake, so why not think about pre-planning their final resting place, their final move? And where better? This cold windy hill was full of people just like themselves—military people and their partners. People who must not have had their own hometown to lie in with relatives in family plots. It *was* a good idea.

So now Michele smiled and hugged Jess, who wondered where all this sentimentality was coming from. Jess had grown up in the eastern Outaouais and had never lived anywhere other than around Ottawa. And she certainly was not thinking about her own burial plot, as young and just starting her own life as she was.

"Geez, Michele, I know you're not coming here, soon, gosh, sorry if I . . . "

"No, Jessica, that's not it. Thank you, I think you're absolutely right. I think Don and I will choose this cemetery for ourselves. It's perfect. Now, let's get the boys and go out for hamburgers."

*A*nd today Don and I still like to go for hikes around Beechwood Cemetery a couple times a year, and try to attend the Wreathes Across Canada yearly ceremony on the first Sunday of December. We always visit our own grave plot and read our names carved into the granite. Sometimes we take pictures of ourselves standing behind the stone. It *doesn't feel morbid; it feels a little like a visit to our future hometown, if you know what I mean!*

Then we go out for hamburgers.

REFLECTION AFTER THE LIFE

It was fun to write a book of memoirs. Aside, that is, from the disturbing nights of dreaming about the past. Most of those dreams were confusing conglomerations of houses and rooms like mazes while I sorted through the memories. Admittedly, this was not what I thought would be the first thing I'd write after retiring from over thirty years in Information Technology, first as a computer programmer at Great-West Life and with the government, then the last twenty as an independent consultant specializing as an Oracle Database Administrator. I made a comfortable living, and raised two okay sons, who rewarded me with wonderful daughters-in-law. I maintained a lasting marriage throughout. I admit I'm proud of my life. So far. The goal was always to write fictional novels—historical and science fiction have always been my favourites. But the darn stories of my own life just kept coming until I "purged the urge" by setting them out together in this book. I hope and expect there's more writing of new kinds to be done after this.

I am old and retired now. Well, not that old, but definitely on chapter next-to-last in the "Big Book" of my life. I look forward to it. Will I ever be a grandmother? What trips can I plan? What more can I do with my writing?

I've lived in Aylmer, Québec now for over two decades, and have no plans to move anywhere else. I do get that restless urge, ingrained from childhood maybe, to at least switch houses once every few years, but usually we just buy a new car when that feeling hits. We can't downsize any more than the condo! I know how to paint a room now. I've settled into a civilian ending to my military beginning.

And honestly, throughout all the twists and fateful meanderings of my early base-brat existence, all the way up to living the rest of my days in my kids' hometown, I've never regretted any of the moves and experiences that living with the military offered in the first, influential half of my life.

My General Panet sweetheart and still love of my life, Don and I still go to our high school reunions every five years in Petawawa. Some of the friends we reconnect with there, we didn't even hang out with back in the day. But those of us who go, do so for the community, the commonality of our upbringing, and the sharing. Because we all shared the experience of having been base brats. No matter where any of us ended up, we all know where we started.

We were Camp Followers.

EPILOGUE

THE SOLDIER

This story is 100% wistful poetic license, except for the memory of a dream by a four year-old in Kingston, Ontario. I still remember that dream.
I can only hope it ends like this.

She wakes to a sound in her ear, somehow familiar, a low growl. It takes a moment to remember where she is. There is thunder rumbling away. The usual sharp hospital whites are blurry, muted; the beeping machines are silent. Slowly, she looks around the room, and, not surprised, she sees her tall, straight soldier beside the closed door, his scarlet tunic bright against the grey walls.

Can it really be almost a *century* since she first saw him? He was her first memory, and then, like now, he had arrived in the after-still of a soft summer storm.

That first, only other time, long years past in Kingston, she had woken to see him in her tiny bedroom. He was just a dream, her mother had said, and true enough, he was gone when her mother looked behind the door. She had been frightened that first time.

She is not afraid today as her soldier walks over to the bed, takes her hand and raises her up. She smiles as he wraps his red-coated arms warmly around her, and then up, up they float, happy, light, and away. She is so looking forward to seeing her mother.

Acknowledgements

I am grateful for the help I received writing this memoir, my first book. I thank these folks for all they contributed.

Don, my first reader. You know what you do for me.

Ken, my father.

Cait Gordon, editor, advisor. So much to learn.

Caro Fréchette, illustrator, advisor. This book became whole with your work.

Éric Desmarais, layout.

My family, sons D'Arcy and Sasha, daughters-in-law Jessica and Janna, who suffered my constant updates and chatter about this book, and even pretended to listen (mostly).

All my other family and friends, ditto.

Most of all, thanks to all readers. I write for you.

About the Author

Michele is retired from careers as a Database Administrator, computer programmer, and lifeguard. She was born in Calgary, Alberta, but grew up on military bases in both Canada and Germany, and now lives with her retired Air Force husband of over 40 years, Don, in Aylmer, Québec. Besides her writing, she loves hiking, sports, music, and travelling. And family.

A reader since her mother first tossed magazines in her crib, she still loves all kinds of books, and will continue writing as either herself, Michele Sabad, or as her author social media persona of Stevie Szabad.

Follow Michele's writing on her author website stevieszabad.com.